THE BOOK OF PSALMS
in Spoken English

A Contemporary Translation
By Rabbi Lazer Brody

Author of:

Three Words of Emuna
Divine Direction
The Worry Worm
The Path to Your Peak
The Language of Emuna
13 Principles of Emuna
Old Isaac's Trail to Tranquility
Bitachon
Chassidic Pearls
The Bond of Emuna
Emuna and the Noahide
The Serene Soul

And other titles

EMUNA BEAMS
Publications

5785 / 2025

Copyright © 2025 by Lazer Brody

All rights reserved. No part of this book may be reproduced in any form without written permission of the author.

No part of this publication may be translated, reproduced, stored in any retrieval system, or transmitted in any form or by any means without prior permission of the author except by a reviewer who wishes to quote brief passages in connection with a review written for inclusion in magazines or newspapers.

In all matters relating to this book, please contact: brody1035@gmail.com

Design and layout by Lieve Maas, Bright Light Graphics, BrightLightGraphics.com

THE BOOK OF PSALMS

in Spoken English

RABBI N. MOSKOWITZ **OF MELITZ** RECHOV HATSIVONY 7/14 ASHDOD, E. ISRAEL	נפתלי א.י. מאסקאוויטש ממעליץ רח' הצבעוני 14/7 טל. 8640028-08 אשדוד

בס"ד _____ אליו תשובה

הסכמה

הן קאי לפני ידידי הותיק ירא ושלם מלאה
וריקים אוהב אלקים ורעים קהילא קדישא אגרה איתן
אאמן חן סופר ווצא. מרקה קלידו. וריקים בעיקר
באביונה דורי אנגליי ואלקים אקלרקים לברסותין
ועת עברים ועונה (אאלומת בנין יהדות. והוך
כי צרכתי קרובל הרדם מאור הלוט לצרוך
תאלים עם כראון קלה וקל כאשר גו וקען יעקידו
אירקה כאור ונלגה כאלות וקאוות ש אוג האלה,
לוך ל ליסוד הגיוון שלי גלגלים שקרא" ובל
חילו האכלים כאיר גל בירשו וחות גא
לבירוש הגאוו, ואתר היקר אגו וצליג שה דוך
סיעם סכונהי ואחתונו אקרים ואקוות ש היהי
לאלת יקו ויקל לים ש שקל אלציו קאומי.
דורי אנגיים הסכמתי יגב הסכי הוא לקים
ולברות לידי הרקי אשאוחו יקראו חים לולא תאלה והודה
ואוועל 3 לן וצולתי באוהה החאט וחסם אמן
/אא. צלו לאת ף

נפ' נפתלי מאסקווי(טש)

(חותם: א.י. מאסקאוויטש — חופ"ק אשדוד — חסד מעליץ)

APPROBATION

Grand Rabbi N. Moskowitz
The Melitzer Rebbe of Ashdod

B"H, Adar, 5785

My longtime friend, the spiritual guide with unblemished reverence of Hashem, Rabbi Eliezer Raphoel (Lazer) Brody, may he merit long life, from our city of Ashdod, came to me with this manuscript. He does much in providing merit to the masses, predominantly in English-speaking countries, with thousands of people listening to his lessons. He also instructs them and answers their questions on subjects related to Jewish faith. In the course of his holy endeavors, he felt an acute need to compile a comprehensible Book of Psalms in contemporary English to enable more people to connect with the Holy One, Blessed be He, in outpouring of the soul by way of the prayers and prayers of King David, may he rest in peace. As the foundation of his translation, he took my elaboration of the Book of Psalms entitled, "Nefesh Chaya," which is mainly based on Rashi's commentary, and he walks on this path here in this translation. After much effort and toil, he succeeded in completing this work. May those who aspire for spiritual understanding take this book. We hope this book will be very beneficial in bringing people's hearts closer to their Father in Heaven.

APPROBATION

I therefore grant my approbation. May this book be distributed throughout the English-speaking world so that many can access the gates of prayer and thanksgiving.

May the virtue of spiritual outreach arouse Divine mercy and compassion so that we see the salvation of Zion and Jerusalem speedily and in our days, amen.

And on this I sign,

Naftali Moskowitz

TABLE OF CONTENTS

Approbation	i
Introduction	xi
Psalm One	3
Psalm Two	4
Psalm Three	6
Psalm Four	8
Psalm Five	10
Psalm Six	12
Psalm Seven	14
Psalm Eight	17
Psalm Nine	19
Psalm Ten	22
Psalm Eleven	25
Psalm Twelve	27
Psalm Thirteen	29
Psalm Fourteen	30
Psalm Fifteen	31
Psalm Sixteen	32
Psalm Seventeen	34
Psalm Eighteen	36
Psalm Nineteen	42
Psalm Twenty	44
Psalm Twenty-One	46
Psalm Twenty-Two	48
Psalm Twenty-Three	52
Psalm Twenty-Four	53
Psalm Twenty-Five	55
Psalm Twenty-Six	58

TABLE OF CONTENTS

Psalm Twenty-Seven	60
Psalm Twenty-Eight	62
Psalm Twenty-Nine	64
Psalm Thirty	66
Psalm Thirty-One	68
Psalm Thirty-Two	71
Psalm Thirty-Three	73
Psalm Thirty-Four	76
Psalm Thirty-Five	79
Psalm Thirty-Six	85
Psalm Thirty-Seven	90
Psalm Thirty-Eight	93
Psalm Thirty-Nine	95
Psalm Forty	98
Psalm Forty-One	100
Psalm Forty-Two	103
Psalm Forty-Three	105
Psalm Forty-Four	106
Psalm Forty-Five	109
Psalm Forty-Six	112
Psalm Forty-Seven	114
Psalm Forty-Eight	116
Psalm Forty-Nine	118
Psalm Fifty	121
Psalm Fifty-One	124
Psalm Fifty-Two	127
Psalm Fifty-Three	129
Psalm Fifty-Four	131
Psalm Fifty-Five	133
Psalm Fifty-Six	136
Psalm Fifty-Seven	138

TABLE OF CONTENTS

Psalm Fifty-Eight	140
Psalm Fifty-Nine	142
Psalm Sixty	145
Psalm Sixty-One	147
Psalm Sixty-Two	148
Psalm Sixty-Three	150
Psalm Sixty-Four	152
Psalm Sixty-Five	154
Psalm Sixty-Six	156
Psalm Sixty-Seven	159
Psalm Sixty-Eight	160
Psalm Sixty-Nine	165
Psalm Seventy	170
Psalm Seventy-One	171
Psalm Seventy-Two	174
Psalm Seventy-Three	179
Psalm Seventy-Four	183
Psalm Seventy-Five	186
Psalm Seventy-Six	188
Psalm Seventy-Seven	190
Psalm Seventy-Eight	193
Psalm Seventy-Nine	201
Psalm Eighty	203
Psalm Eighty-One	206
Psalm Eighty-Two	208
Psalm Eighty-Three	209
Psalm Eighty-Four	212
Psalm Eighty-Five	214
Psalm Eighty-Six	216
Psalm Eighty-Seven	218
Psalm Eighty-Eight	219

TABLE OF CONTENTS

Psalm Eighty-Nine	222
Psalm Ninety	231
Psalm Ninety-One	234
Psalm Ninety-Two	236
Psalm Ninety-Three	238
Psalm Ninety-Four	239
Psalm Ninety-Five	242
Psalm Ninety-Six	244
Psalm Ninety-Seven	246
Psalm Ninety-Eight	248
Psalm Ninety-Nine	250
Psalm One Hundred	252
Psalm One Hundred One	253
Psalm One Hundred Two	255
Psalm One Hundred Three	259
Psalm One Hundred Four	262
Psalm One Hundred Five	266
Psalm One Hundred Six	272
Psalm One Hundred Seven	281
Psalm One Hundred Eight	286
Psalm One Hundred Nine	288
Psalm One Hundred Ten	292
Psalm One Hundred Eleven	294
Psalm One Hundred Twelve	296
Psalm One Hundred Thirteen	298
Psalm One Hundred Fourteen	299
Psalm One Hundred Fifteen	301
Psalm One Hundred Sixteen	303
Psalm One Hundred Seventeen	305
Psalm One Hundred Eighteen	306
Psalm One Hundred Nineteen	310

TABLE OF CONTENTS

Psalm One Hundred Twenty	328
Psalm One Hundred Twenty-One	330
Psalm One Hundred Twenty-Two	331
Psalm One Hundred Twenty-Three	333
Psalm One Hundred Twenty-Four	334
Psalm One Hundred Twenty-Five	335
Psalm One Hundred Twenty-Six	336
Psalm One Hundred Twenty-Seven	337
Psalm One Hundred Twenty-Eight	338
Psalm One Hundred Twenty-Nine	339
Psalm One Hundred Thirty	340
Psalm One Hundred Thirty-One	341
Psalm One Hundred Thirty-Two	342
Psalm One Hundred Thirty-Three	345
Psalm One Hundred Thirty-Four	346
Psalm One Hundred Thirty-Five	347
Psalm One Hundred Thirty-Six	350
Psalm One Hundred Thirty-Seven	353
Psalm One Hundred Thirty-Eight	355
Psalm One Hundred Thirty-Nine	357
Psalm One Hundred Forty	360
Psalm One Hundred Forty-One	362
Psalm One Hundred Forty-Two	364
Psalm One Hundred Forty-Three	366
Psalm One Hundred Forty-Four	368
Psalm One Hundred Forty-Five	370
Psalm One Hundred Forty-Six	373
Psalm One Hundred Forty-Seven	375
Psalm One Hundred Forty-Eight	378
Psalm One Hundred Forty-Nine	380
Psalm One Hundred Fifty	382

INTRODUCTION

With the Almighty's infinite grace, we joyously present "The Book of Psalms in Spoken English." Why "spoken English" rather than "plain" or "contemporary" English? The psalms are meant to be vocalized, whether sung or recited. Rebbe Nachman of Breslov teaches that the voice arouses the heart, even if that voice is a whisper, inaudible to the person standing right next to you.

Nothing is so conducive to arousing the heart as King David's Psalms are. We therefore have prepared an original translation in spoken English to make the psalms more meaningful and accessible to people from all backgrounds.

From Heart to Heart
The Zohar teaches us a firm law in spirituality: an arousal of the human heart in the material world creates an equivalent arousal of the Divine heart in the spiritual realm. For that reason, the Levites in the Holy Temple would sing the songs of David, better known as psalms. Both the words and the melodies would inspire them beyond description, thus enhancing the intensity and sincerity of their prayers. Where did that power of inspiration come from originally?

David's songs brought tremendous gratification to the "Divine heart," the Kabbalistic metaphor known as the

INTRODUCTION

lev elyon. This, in turn, refers to the *ratzon elyon*, or Divine Will. Divine Will is essentially the apex of Godliness, the sphere of *Keter*, the Divine crown.

Rabbi Shlomo Hakohen Rabinowitz of Radomsk (1801-1866) adds that the sincere words said from the human heart are capable of penetrating the Divine heart (Tiferes Shlomo, Parshas Truma).

Protocols of Personal Prayers

Rebbe Nachman of Breslov (1772-1810) notes that The Book of Psalms is the protocols of 150 intimate personal prayers that David sang to the Almighty. These prayers were infused with *ruach haKodesh,* a spirit of holiness that is tantamount to prophecy (see Likutei Moharan I:156).

King David would sing his prayers using a number of musical instruments. Yet sometimes, his prayers were vocal only, simple cries from the depth of his soul. David's songs penetrated the Divine heart because they came from the depths of his own heart.

The Inclusive Soul

Rabbi Avraham Weinberg of Slonim (1803-1883) writes that Moshiach, the anointed King of Israel, has an "inclusive soul" that includes the sparks of all the souls of all generations (Yesod Ha'avoda, Part 2, Letter 47). This concept is further validated in Chassidic sources. Rabbi Menachem Nachum Twersky of Chernobyl (1730-1797) says that the baton of "inclusive souls" began with Adam, then passed on to King David, who was the anointed King of Israel, and finally to Moshiach (Messiah), may he come soon, amen. In fact, "Adam" is an acronym of A'dam, D'avid and M'oshiach.

Inclusive Suffering

No one in history, not even Job, can compete with King David regarding suffering. David's brothers despised him. His father mistakenly thought that he was an illegitimate child. As such, the family cast him out into the wilderness as a little boy to tend their flocks. They hoped a wild animal would devour the tender lad, who in their eyes was a disgrace to the family. That's why David had to battle lions and bears to survive (see Samuel I, 17:36).

What child, alone in the wilderness at midnight with the hooting of owls and the howling of wolves and jackals, wouldn't be consumed by fear? From a tender age, King David put all his trust in Hashem and called out to Him. He maintained this level of trust his entire life, even as a mighty warrior and all-powerful king. Nonetheless, he describes himself as "…a child in his mother's arms" (Psalm 131:2).

As a young Bar Mitzvah boy, King David confronted the colossal Goliath. Just seeing the gigantic brute and hearing his deafening threats and epithets could cause anyone a heart attack. David's wife, Michal, disparaged him, and his father-in-law, King Saul, tried to kill him. Not one but two sons— Avshalom and Adoniahu—revolted against him. Achitopel, his closest advisor, betrayed him. Highly influential peers such as Doeg the Edomite plotted endlessly against him and defamed King David at every opportunity.

INTRODUCTION

King David had every sort of enemy, internal and external. He fought every sort of battle. At one point, in Ziklag, his own soldiers blamed him for their troubles and almost revolted against him (see Samuel I: Ch. 30). The Amalekites kidnapped his wife Avigail, whom he especially loved (ibid). He was exiled on multiple occasions. What's more, King David suffered a six-month bout with leprosy (see Sanhedrin 107a). As a fugitive, he suffered hunger and thirst. And the list is not yet complete…

Why did Hashem make David suffer like this?

The All-Inclusive Remedy

King David suffered every type of tribulation and suffering. Since his faith was unwavering, he knew that everything came from Hashem. He therefore prayed to Hashem for his every need. He relied on Hashem for every solution, remedy, deliverance, and success. He consequently describes himself in two words, *va'ani tefillah* – "and I am prayer" (Psalm 109:4). Prayer was the entire essence of King David, and the psalms are the essence of his prayers.

As the "all-inclusive" soul, King David's soul was a kaleidoscope of all our souls. His suffering was a compendium of all of our suffering. David's song, his Book of Psalms, is therefore our song, for every person on earth for posterity. Each one of us can find ourselves in the Book of Psalms. It expresses our pain and our aspirations. It describes our trials and our tribulations. No wonder that the Book of Psalms is by far history's greatest best-seller.

INTRODUCTION

Rebbe Nachman of Breslov urges us to recite the psalms sincerely, with all our heart. So much so, that tears should well up in our eyes (Likutei Moharan II: 95). When a person says the psalms with sincerity, he or she can literally find themselves and their own circumstances within the psalms (ibid, 101).

Penetrating the Heart

Furthermore, as Rebbe Nachman writes elsewhere (ibid., 25), a person's discourse with the Almighty "should be in the language one normally uses, one's native tongue, because it is difficult for a person to say everything he wants to say in the Holy Tongue. Also, being unfamiliar with that language, one's heart is not moved by the words, as we are not accustomed to speaking Hebrew. But in our native tongue, in which we normally speak and converse, it is much easier and so more likely for one to penetrate the heart. This is because the heart is drawn to a person's native tongue and closer to it, because of his familiarity with it."

Rebbe Nachman's above concept was a prime source of motivation in this translation. Words that the reader understands penetrate the heart, and words that penetrate the heart have the power to arouse and inspire. This is our main incentive in bringing "The Book of Psalms in Spoken English" to contemporary English speakers.

Understanding and Sincerity

King David's Psalms in their original *lashon hakodesh*, literally "the holy tongue" or Biblical Hebrew, are beyond persuasive. First of all, he sings them in the language of the Torah. And second, the language of the Torah is very spiritual. English,

INTRODUCTION

on the other hand, is a very material-oriented language. The English lexicon sorely lacks spiritual terms. Therefore, one cannot accurately convey the power and flavor of King David's message without understanding the intent of the message.

Take this classic translation of Psalm 128:1 for example: "Happy is every one that feareth the LORD, that walketh in His ways." What 21st Century English speaker could say such a passage sincerely? What does it mean to "fear?" That, of course, is a literal translation of the Hebrew word *yarei*. Does that obligate us to tremble in fear all day long? How can a person be happy if he or she is afraid that a bolt of lightning will hit them in the head at any moment? That was certainly not King David's intention.

Within the limitations of English vocabulary, *yarei* would better be translated as "awe" or "revere", an emotion that describes extreme admiration and respect. When we think of awe, we conjure wide-open gaping eyes and a mouth agape, like witnessing the Northern Lights in Norway or a shower of meteors in the desert sky. When we think of "revere", we imagine how we'd feel if we met King David or Elijah the Prophet face to face.

With the above in mind, I would opt for a fluid translation that is also an interpretation in contemporary spoken English and say, "Happy is any person who reveres Hashem and walks in His ways."

Imminent threats that evoke strong fear have nothing to do with David's intention of exalting God, revering Him and holding Him in awe. Since simplicity and clarity are the two goals of this translation, we preferred the use of "revere" rather than awe. Whereas "revere" and "reverence" have the connotation of awe coupled with deep belief, "awe" and "awesome" in spoken English are sorely overused. This is just one example of the painstaking efforts we have made to translate each word with King David's true intention.

Proper Translation and Interpretation

Clarity, simplicity and understanding are requisites of sincerity. Proper translation according to *pshat*, the basic interpretation, meaning and intent of a passage, is a requisite to truth. *Pshat* comes from the Hebrew word *pashut*, which means "simple."

One of history's greatest Biblical translation blunders led to the antisemitic myth that Jews have horns. How so? Michelangelo sculpted his famous statue of Moses and placed a pair of horns on his head. This came from a mistranslation of Exodus 34:30. How?

Moses came down from Mount Sinai after spending forty days and nights in the Divine Presence. His face, therefore, emanated dazzling, nearly blinding rays of Divine light. The Torah says, *v'hinei karan ohr panav*, or "behold, his face sent forth rays." The Hebrew word *karan* is the verb of *keren*, which has two meanings: a ray of light or a horn.

The Latin translation of our holy Torah that Michelangelo depended on was a verbatim translation that utterly lacked understanding and context. As such, the non-Jewish and

INTRODUCTION

untraditional translations of the Tanach in general and the Book of Psalms in particular are inaccurate, misleading, and outright mistaken. In the case of Exodus 34:30, the Latin translation reads, "behold, his face sent forth horns." This horrendous mistake in translation has become the authoritative source of antisemites for centuries that Jews have horns.

"Nefesh Chaya", the Elaborated Psalms

To make the Book of Psalms more accessible and comprehendible to modern Hebrew speakers, my esteemed teacher Grand Rabbi Naftali A.Y. Moscowitz shlit'a, aka the Melitzer Rebbe of Ashdod, wrote an elaboration on the Book of Psalms entitled "Nefesh Chaya." This monumental project was in memory of his oldest daughter, Rebbetzen Chaya Mirl Golla Leiffer, osb'm, who passed away as a young mother from a terminal disease.

This elaboration is primarily based on the Rashi (acronym for Rabbi Shlomo Yitzchaki, 1040-1105) commentary, the most accurate and authoritative interpretation of the Book of Psalms.

The "Nefesh Chaya" Book of Psalms has become immensely popular both in Israel and in Torah circles abroad. A gift to the contemporary Hebrew speaker, it has been reprinted multiple times since it first appeared in 5758 (1998). By helping Modern Hebrew speakers to better understand what they're saying, the "Nefesh Chaya" Book of Psalms plays a key role in enhancing sincerity and enthusiasm. With enhanced clarity, people can readily pray from the heart.

INTRODUCTION

The Book of Psalms in Spoken English

The old expression says that if you want something done, do it yourself. As I would recite psalms from my copy of "Nefesh Chaya", I'd often ponder how wonderful it would be for the modern English speaker to have access to this remarkable text.

Again, I use the word "recite" in the previous paragraph rather than "read." Psalms are meant to be recited, whether audibly or in a whisper. By way of our spoken psalms, we gain the golden opportunity to express ourselves from the heart and speak to Hashem when we might otherwise be tongue-tied.

I therefore asked the Melitzer Rebbe shlit'a for permission and his blessing to translate King David's prodigiously holy Book of Psalms while using the "Nefesh Chaya" as my main—but not exclusive—source of *pshat*. He readily agreed so that English speakers, too, can gain access to a meaningful and accurate translation of psalms.

There were times when my understanding of *pshat* of a particular word or passage differed from the Rebbe's understanding. I would come to the Rebbe with citations from classical interpretations, such as that of the *Radak* (Rabbi David Kimhi, 1160–1235), the ibn Ezra (1089-1167) and the *Metzudas David* (Rabbi David Altschuler, 1687-1769); as these commentaries differed from Rashi, they differed from the "Nefesh Chaya" as well.

The Melitzer Rebbe, in his extreme humility, Torah integrity, and quest for truth, encouraged me to disagree with his Rashi-based interpretation when I had strong backing from

INTRODUCTION

other classical sources to support my way of understanding King David's intention. I cannot thank the Rebbe shlit'a enough for his guidance, time, and patience over the course of this project.

This translation is "The Book of Psalms in Spoken English." We have taken the liberty of going beyond translation. For the sake of clarity and facilitated understanding, our translations are also interpretations in attempt to accurately convey King David's intent. We have also footnoted relevant passages from the Torah, Prophets, and Scripture that provide background for a particular psalm and the circumstances of its composition.

The Almighty's Holy Name

According to the Melitzer Rebbe's instructions, we translate The Ineffable Name (the four Hebrew letters yud-hey-vav-hay) as "Hashem", which literally means *the Name*. The Name aleph-daled-nun-yud (A-donoi) appears here as "Lord" and the name aleph-lamed-hey-yud-mem (E'lohim) is referred to as "God".

* * *

For the sake of clarity, this translation also relies heavily on the *Targum*, the classic Tannaic-period translation of psalms into Aramaic.

Just as "there is no grain without the chaff" (Nedarim 8a), there is no book without mistakes. We have tried our utmost to honor and preserve the holiness and intent of King David's

INTRODUCTION

monumental Psalms, painstakingly treating each word like a priceless gemstone. Our prayers for guidance and accuracy in this huge endeavor are virtually embedded in every verse. Still, most probably, there may be mistakes. We therefore ask forgiveness from Hashem, from King David, from the Melitzer Rebbe shlit'a, and from you, esteemed reader.

May it be Hashem's will that "The Book of Psalms in Spoken English" make it easier, more meaningful, and more enjoyable for people of all backgrounds to pour their hearts out to the Almighty and develop an intimate relationship with Him. This book is for you, dear English speaker, no matter who you are or where you are. May the Almighty protect you, comfort you, answer all your prayers, and grant you all your heart's wishes for the very best, amen.

With every blessing and in eager anticipation of hearing the Songs of David in our rebuilt Holy Temple in Jerusalem,

Rabbi Lazer Brody, Ashdod, Israel,
Sivan, 5785 / June, 2025

BOOK ONE

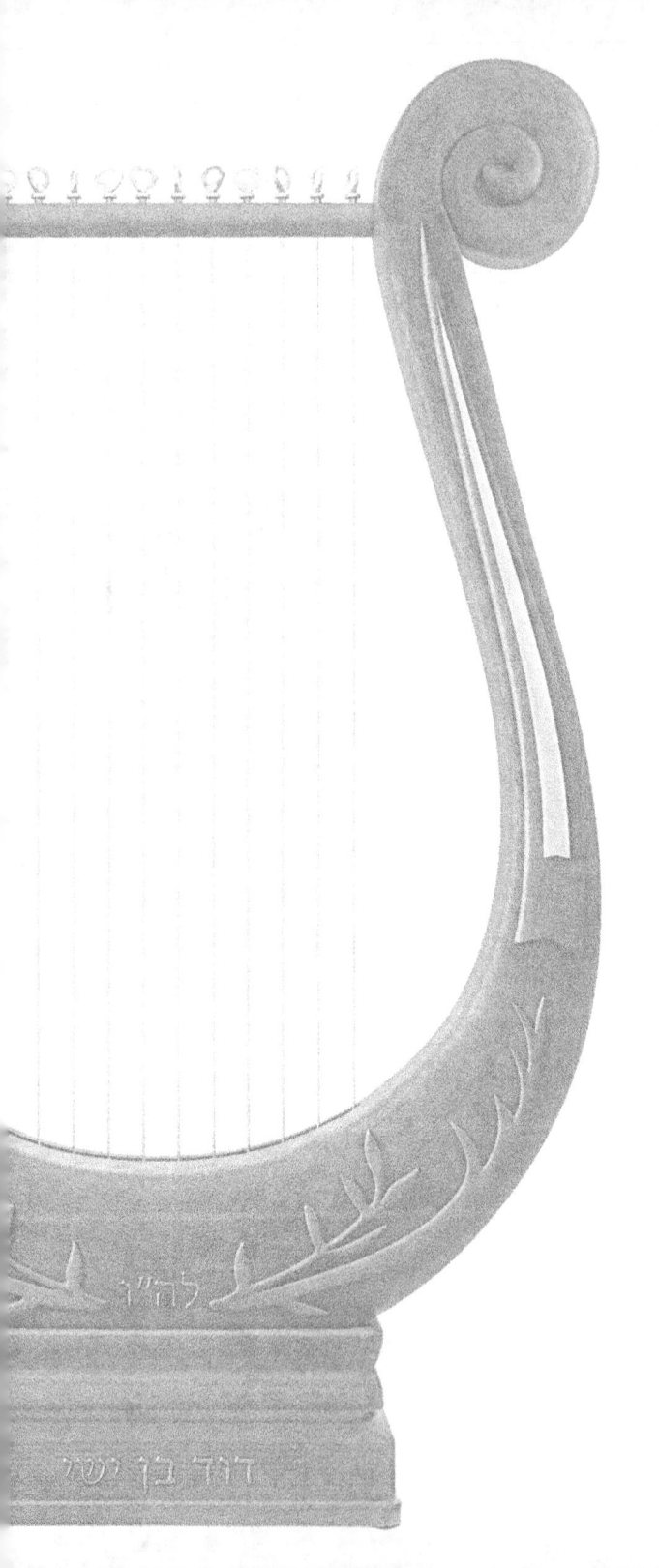

PSALM ONE

The good fortune of the righteous and the fate of the wicked

1. Happy is the man who never followed the ways of the wicked, nor joined with transgressors, nor sat among scoffers.

2. Instead, he desires Hashem's teachings and contemplates His Torah, day and night.

3. And he'll be like a tree planted by a riverbank, yielding its fruit in season, with leaves that never wilt; and everything he does will succeed.

4. Not so the wicked, who are like chaff blown by the wind.

5. Therefore, the evildoers will not prevail on judgment day, and the sinners won't be allowed in the domain of the righteous.

6. For Hashem rewards the ways of the righteous, but the ways of the wicked lead to oblivion.

PSALM TWO

Hashem's anger at the nations for rising up against Him

1. Why are the nations in an uproar? Why do the people of the world plot in vain?

2. The kings of the earth and the nobles gather together to plot against Hashem and the one He anointed.

3. "Let us free ourselves of His reign and sever all ties with Him."

4. The Almighty in heaven laughs and mocks them.

5. He'll then speak to them in anger; His displeasure will terrify them.

6. "For I Am the One Who crowned My king over Zion, My holy mountain."

7. I am obliged to tell what Hashem said to me: "You are My son; for Me, today is like the day of your birth;

8. simply ask Me and I will give you nations as your inheritance and the far corners of the earth for your possession."

PSALM TWO

9   You will smash them with an iron rod and shatter them like pottery.

10   So now, you monarchs, come to your senses; you magistrates, be warned.

11   Serve Hashem with reverence and rejoice with trembling.

12   Purify your hearts or else you'll kindle His wrath and be doomed; for in an instant, His anger will blaze. Happy are the people who take refuge in Him.

PSALM THREE

A prayer to Hashem to be rescued from enemies

1. A psalm by David, when he fled from his son Absalom:[1]

2. God, I have so many enemies! Powerful people rise up against me.

3. Many tell me that my soul stands no chance of salvation from the Lord.

4. But You, Hashem, are my protective shield and my dignity; You uplift my head.

5. I will always call out to Hashem and He will answer me from His holy mountain.

6. I lay down in troubled sleep, yet I awake encouraged, for Hashem holds me up.

7. I will not fear the many adversaries that surround me.

---

1   For the background of this psalm, see II Samuel, 15:30

PSALM THREE

8 Rise up, Hashem! Save me, my God! For You have struck all my enemies in the face and have shattered the teeth of the wicked.

9 Salvation comes from Hashem; may You bestow Your blessing on Your nation forever.

PSALM FOUR

A plea to Hashem for rescue from the straits of hatred and slander

1. For the conductor of the Temple orchestra, a psalm by David:

2. When I call, answer me, my charitable God; in the straits of sorrow, You have brought me relief; be gracious to me and hear my prayer.

3. You mortals, how long will you trample my dignity, love what is futile, and chase after falsehood?

4. Know that Hashem has set apart the pious person for Himself; Hashem will hear when I call Him.

5. Tremble and don't sin; reflect in your hearts while lying in bed and forever remain silent.

6. Let your good deeds be your offering, and trust in Hashem.

7. Many say, "Who will show us the good life? Let the light of Your face shine upon us, Hashem!"

PSALM FOUR

8   The joy You have put in my heart is greater than the joy of the nations when they harvest an abundance of grain and wine.

9   When there is peace, I will both lie down and sleep, for You, Hashem, enable me to dwell securely in solitude.

PSALM FIVE

A plea for one's prayers to be answered and to be beyond the reach of evil and fraudulent people

1. For the conductor of the Temple ensemble, a psalm by David:

2. Listen to my words, Hashem; look at the intent of my heart.

3. Heed the sound of my prayer, my God and my King, for I pray to You alone.

4. Hashem, hear my voice in the morning; as each morning, I will plead to You and wait with hope.

5. For You are not a god[2] who desires wickedness; evil cannot reside with You.

---

2. Rashi and other classic interpretations of Psalms are inconclusive whether this name is holy or not. After consulting with the Melitzer Rebbe shlit'a, we translated this in the mundane form, meaning that King David is telling Hashem that He is not like the false gods who condone evil rituals and people. Therefore, we wrote "god" with a lower-case letter g. Throughout Tana'ch, there are numerous other similar names that are *safeq*, doubtful if they are holy or mundane. A very similar example is Deuteronomy 32:21.

PSALM FIVE

6 Shameless fools cannot endure in Your sight; You despise those who do evil.

7 You will doom the liars; Hashem despises murderous and deceitful people.

8 But I, with Your abundant compassion, will enter Your house; in admiration of You, I will bow down at Your Holy Sanctuary.

9 Hashem, guide me along the path of Your righteousness because of those who seek to subdue me; give me direct access to Your way.

10 For there is no sincerity in their mouth; their hearts are full of malice; and their throats are an open grave; they are smooth talkers.

11 Declare them guilty, O God; may they fall into their own traps; repel them because of their many crimes, for they have rebelled against You.

12 Let all who take refuge in You rejoice; they will sing forever as You shelter them; let those who love Your Name exult in You.

13 For You will bless the righteous, Hashem; You will surround them with goodness like a shield.

PSALM SIX

Arousing Hashem's mercy from the depths of sickness and trouble

1. For the conductor of the Temple orchestra: on the eight-string lyre, a psalm by David:

2. Hashem, do not rebuke me in Your anger nor discipline me in Your wrath.

3. Have mercy on me, Hashem, for I am weak; heal me, Hashem, for my bones tremble in fear.

4. My soul is deeply shaken; and You, Hashem, how long will You refuse to cure me?

5. Come back, Hashem, rescue my soul! Save me, for the sake of Your lovingkindness.

6. For in death, there is no mention of You; from the grave, who will praise You?

7. I am weary from my groaning; every night, my bed is soaking wet, drenched with my tears.

8. My eyes have dimmed from aggravation; they've grown old because of my tormentors.

PSALM SIX

9   Go away from me, all you deceivers, for Hashem has heard the sound of my weeping.

10 Hashem has heard my plea; Hashem will accept my prayer.

11 Let my enemies be shamed and utterly shocked; they will turn back and be humiliated in an instant.

PSALM SEVEN

A plea for rescue from tormentors, that they fall into the trap they set for others

1. David's song of remorse that he sang to Hashem regarding Cush[3] from the tribe of Benjamin.

2. Hashem, my God, I seek refuge in You; deliver me from those who torment me and rescue me.

3. Otherwise, he'll devour my soul like a lion, ripping me apart with no one to rescue me.

4. Hashem, my God, have I done wrong? Are my hands guilty of wrongdoing?

5. Have I acted vengefully toward those who were at peace with me? Did I not release my tormentor without harming him?[4]

---

3 A reference to King Saul, who came from the Tribe of Benjamin; on numerous occasions, he attempted to kill David (see I Samuel, chapters 18-19).

4 On two occasions, David could have killed Saul but refused to do so (see I Samuel 24:2-8 and 26:5-11).

PSALM SEVEN

6   If I am guilty, let my enemy chase me down, overtake me, and trample my life into the ground; let him bury my soul in the dust forever.

7   Rise up, Hashem, in Your fury against my tormentors; and gloriously awaken judgment against them by the laws You commanded.

8   When the nations of the world seek Your help, rise far above them and return to the heavens.

9   Hashem, prosecute the nations; judge me according to my righteousness and integrity.

10   Let the wicked fall by their own evil deeds and let the righteous flourish, for God examines their hearts and minds.

11   I rely on God for protection, for He rescues those with upright hearts.

12   God is the righteous judge, and He is angered by the wicked every day.

13   If one doesn't mend his ways, He will sharpen His sword and His bow, taking aim at him.

14   Against the wicked, He has prepared deadly weapons; He will shoot His arrows against those who pursue the righteous.

PSALM SEVEN

15 Notice how the evil person conceives wickedness, is pregnant with conniving, and gives birth to falsehood.

16 He has dug a deep pit, and ultimately falls into the trap of his own making.

17 His evil scheme will boomerang right back at his own head, and his own violence will crash down on his skull.

18 I will thank Hashem for His righteous judgment and will sing praise to the supreme Name of Hashem.

PSALM EIGHT

Hashem's greatness in empowering feeble humans

1. For the conductor of the Temple orchestra: on the lyre from Gat, a psalm by David:

2. Hashem, our Lord, how mighty is Your Name throughout the earth, as Your glory presides over the heavens.

3. From the prayers of the unborn and little babies, You formed the strength to neutralize tormentors and to avenge the enemy.

4. When I gaze at the heavens, the work of Your fingers, the moon and stars that You have created.

5. What is man, that You are mindful of him? What is the human being, that You care for him?

6. Yet, You made him only slightly lower than the angels, and You crowned him with dignity and splendor.

7. You let him reign over the creations of Your hands and have placed everything beneath his feet.

8. Sheep and cattle, all of them, and even wild beasts.

PSALM EIGHT

9   The birds of the sky and the fish in the sea; for he even traverses the seas.

10   Hashem, our Lord, how mighty is Your Name throughout the earth!

PSALM NINE

A prayer for the downfall of evil and that Hashem uplift His downtrodden people

1. For the conductor, a psalm by David, when the sins of Israel's youth will be absolved:

2. I thank Hashem with all my heart; I will speak of Your wondrous deeds.

3. I will rejoice and revel in You and will sing praise to Your supreme Name.

4. When my enemies retreat, they will encounter You, then stumble and perish.

5. Because You have judged me and declared my innocence; You have sat on Your throne, righteous Judge!

6. You chastised nations and destroyed the wicked; You obliterated their name forever and ever.

7. The ruins of the enemy are gone forever; You demolished their cities and destroyed any memory of them.

PSALM NINE

8. Hashem reigns forever and prepares His throne for judgment.

9. He will judge the world in righteousness and will give the nations a fair trial.

10. Hashem will be a fortress for the oppressed, a fortress in times of trouble.

11. Those who know Your Name will trust in You, for You have not abandoned those who seek You, Hashem.

12. Sing praise to Hashem, Who dwells in Zion; tell the nations about His magnificent deeds.

13. He avenges the blood of the innocent, remembers them, and does not forget the cry of the humble.

14. Have mercy on me, Hashem; see how those who hate me torment me; uplift me from the gates of death,

15. so I can tell of Your glory at the gates of Zion; I will rejoice in Your salvation.

16. The nations fell into their own pit; their feet were caught in the very same trap that they set for me.

17. Hashem reveals Himself through His judgments; the work of His hands causes the downfall of the evil; and we will tell this forever.

PSALM NINE

18 The wicked will return to the deepest grave, all the nations that forget Hashem.

19 The needy will not be forgotten forever, the hope of the humble will not be lost forever.

20 Arise, Hashem, do not let the wicked mortal become more powerful; let the nations stand trial before You.

21 Hashem, cast Your judgment upon them; let them forever know that they are only mortals.

PSALM TEN

A prayer for the victims of tyranny and tyrants

1. Why do You stand afar, Hashem, and conceal Yourself in times of distress?

2. In his arrogance, the evil person hunts down the poor, who are ensnared in the schemes that the evil people devise.

3. The evil person praises himself for attaining what he wants, and the robber applauds himself for angering Hashem.

4. Because of his arrogance, the evil person will not seek Hashem; all his sinister thoughts tell him that there is no God.

5. He succeeds every time that Your justice seems to disregard him; he repels his enemies with a puff of his mouth.

6. The evil one tells himself that he'll never stumble and never encounter adversity.

7. He swears falsely, his mouth is full of deception, and his tongue harbors wickedness and lies.

PSALM TEN

8   He lies in his nook of ambush to kill the innocent in concealed places; he spies on the destitute.

9   Like a lion, he lurks in ambush from his hiding place; he prowls to seize the poor person, then drags him in his net.

10 He lowers himself, crouches, then pounces with his might on the unfortunate.

11 He tells himself, "God has forgotten; He hid His face; He will never see."

12 Arise, Hashem! God, lift Your hand; do not forget the humble!

13 Why does the wicked person anger God? He tells himself that You don't pay attention to what he does.

14 But You do see what he does! You do observe criminal and anger-provoking acts; everything is in Your power; let the downtrodden depend on You. You have always helped the orphan.

15 Break the power of the wicked person; punish him for his evil until no more is found.

16 Hashem is King forever and ever; the nations vanished from His land.

PSALM TEN

17 You have heard the wish of the meek, Hashem; strengthen their hearts in prayer and listen to them.

18 Judge the orphan and the oppressed; may there be no more tyranny against a single human on earth.

PSALM ELEVEN

Hashem's loathing of the wicked and His love for the righteous

1 For the conductor, by David: I have taken refuge in Hashem; how can you tell my soul to flee from the mountain like a bird?

2 See how the wicked draw their bow,[5] preparing their arrows on the bowstring to shoot in the dark at the upright of heart.

3 If the foundations are destroyed,[6] what has the righteous person done wrong?

4 Even though Hashem is in His holy abode, His Throne in Heaven, His eyes see and scrutinize all of humanity.

5 Hashem tests the righteous but loathes the wicked and the lover of violence.

---

5 This is a reference to the people of Keila; after David rescued them from the Philistines, instead of thanking him, they informed King Saul of his whereabouts, forcing David to Ziph; the Ziphites also betrayed him (see I Samuel, Ch. 23).

6 The "foundations" are the righteous who are the foundations of the world; in this case, David is referring to the holy priests of Nob, who were killed after Doeg the Edomite informed King Saul that they sheltered David (see I Samuel, Ch. 22).

PSALM ELEVEN

6   He will pour hot coals on the wicked; fire, brimstone, and scorching winds are the portion in their cup.

7   For Hashem is righteous and He loves righteousness; the upright will bask in the light of His face.

PSALM TWELVE

A prayer to uproot those with malicious tongues and to protect their victims

1. For the conductor, on the eight-string lyre, a psalm by David:

2. Help, Hashem! For the righteous person has become extinct because faithfulness has disappeared from humanity.

3. People lie to each other, with smooth talk on their lips and deceit in their hearts.

4. May Hashem sever the smooth-talking lips and the arrogant tongues.

5. They say that they can raise their voices and say what they please because no one can tell them what to do.

6. Because of the plundered poor and the cry of the destitute, "Now, I shall arise," says Hashem; "I will lead him to safety in an instant."

7. Hashem's words are pure like purified silver, apparent to the world, refined seven times over.

PSALM TWELVE

8 You will guard the destitute, Hashem; protect them from such a generation forever;

9 Where the wicked walk on all sides and mankind praises vulgarity.

PSALM THIRTEEN

Strengthening trust in Hashem

1. For the conductor, a psalm by David:

2. Hashem, will You forget me forever? How long will You hide Your face from me?

3. How long must I seek ways to rid myself of the grief that fills my heart each day? How long will my enemy prevail over me?

4. See me and answer my prayer, Hashem, my God! Illuminate my eyes so I don't fall into the sleep of death,

5. or else my enemy will boast that he has overcome me, and my tormentors rejoice in my collapse.

6. But I will trust in Your lovingkindness; my heart will rejoice in Your salvation; I will sing to Hashem, for He has dealt bountifully with me.

PSALM FOURTEEN

A prayer for salvation

1. For the conductor, by David: The rogue says in his heart, "There is no God!" People's actions are corrupt, disgusting, and devoid of good.

2. Hashem looks down from heaven to see if there is any astute individual who seeks God.

3. They have all gone astray; together, they've become corrupt; not a single one of them does good.

4. Don't they understand, all these evil people? They devour My people like bread; they don't call to Hashem.

5. There, they will tremble in fear, for God is with the righteous generation.

6. You ridicule the poor person's trust in Hashem.

7. May we witness from Zion the redemption of Israel! When Hashem returns His people from captivity, Jacob will rejoice, and Israel will rejoice.

PSALM FIFTEEN

The virtues of the righteous who are worthy of basking in Hashem's Presence

1. A psalm by David: Hashem, who is worthy of residing in Your Tabernacle? Who may dwell on Your holy mountain?

2. One whose ways are unblemished, who acts justly and speaks truth sincerely.

3. His tongue is devoid of slander; he has not harmed anyone, nor has he disgraced his neighbor.

4. He despises despicable people but honors those who revere Hashem; he'll swear to keep his oath even when it hurts.

5. He does not lend money with interest, nor has he accepted a bribe against the innocent; one who acts accordingly will never falter.

PSALM SIXTEEN

A prayer for Divine protection

1. David's sonnet: protect me, Hashem, for I have taken refuge in You.

2. You, my soul, said to Hashem, "You are my Lord; You are the good in my life."

3. All my desires are fulfilled through the merit of the holy ones who are buried in the earth.

4. May the sorrow of idolators deepen, those who chase after false gods; I will neither offer their blood libations nor allow their names on my lips.

5. Hashem is my portion and the share in my cup; You uplift my destiny.

6. My allotment has come to me in pleasant places; even my inheritance is lovely.

7. I will bless Hashem Who has advised me; even my conscience admonishes me at night.

8. I envision Hashem with me always; He stands to my right to prevent me from stumbling.

PSALM SIXTEEN

9   Therefore, my heart will rejoice, my soul will delight, and my body will dwell in security.

10   For You will not abandon my soul to the nether world nor will You let Your pious see decay.

11   Enlighten me in the path of life that brings me to complete joy in Your Presence, the eternal bliss at Your right hand.

PSALM SEVENTEEN

A prayer for Hashem's mercy and for the downfall of enemies

1. David's prayer: hear, Hashem! Listen to my earnest prayer; be attentive to my prayer from lips devoid of deceit.

2. May my judgment come forth from You and may Your eyes witness my honesty.

3. You examined my heart; You have visited me at night; You have purified me, but You did not find a single thought unworthy of vocalizing.

4. As for Your commandments regarding the deeds of man, I have guarded myself from the ways of anarchy.

5. Help me stride along Your designated paths so that my feet will not falter.

6. I called out to You because You will answer me; God, be mindful of me and hear my prayer.

7. May Your acts of lovingkindness be evident; let Your merciful hand rescue those who seek refuge from assailants.

8. Protect me like the pupil of the eye; conceal me in the shadow of Your Presence.

9. Protect me from these evil people who rob me, the deadly enemies that surround me.

10. Their fat clogs their heart; their mouths speak in arrogance.

11. The moment we take a step, they surround us; they monitor our every move to see where they can trap us.

12. Each of them resembles a lion craving to devour its prey; like a young lion lurking from a hideout.

13. Arise, Hashem! Confront and overcome him; by Your sword, rescue my soul from the evil one.

14. May I be among those who die by Your hand, Hashem; among those who die of old age, whose portion is eternal life, where You will fill them with Your hidden treasures; they will be satiated with offspring and will bequeath their abundance to their children.

15. As for me, in righteousness, I shall behold Your face; when I awake, Your image will satiate me.

PSALM EIGHTEEN

David's praise of Hashem for rescuing him from all his enemies

1. For the conductor, a song by Hashem's servant David that he spoke on the day that Hashem delivered him from the hand of all his enemies and from the hand of Saul.

2. I love You, Hashem, my source of strength.

3. Hashem is my Rock, my Fortress and my Rescuer; I will trust in my steadfast God; He is my shield and my source of salvation Who uplifts me.

4. I call out to Hashem in praise, and I'll be saved from my enemies.

5. The agony of death enveloped me, and torrents of godless men terrorized me.

6. The agony of the grave surrounded me; snares of death confronted me.

7. In anguish, I would call out to Hashem; I would cry out to my God; from His sanctuary, He would hear my voice, and my plea would reach His ears.

PSALM EIGHTEEN

8   And the earth quaked and resounded, and the foundations of the mountains trembled; they quaked because of His wrath.

9   Smoke arose from His nostrils, an all-consuming fire came from His mouth; burning coals blazed from Him.

10 He bent the heavens and descended with a dark fog beneath His feet.

11 He rode on an angel and flew; He soared on the wings of the wind.

12 He made darkness His hideout and enveloped Himself in a shelter of dark waters and thick clouds of the heavens.

13 From His brilliant reflection, His clouds passed over with hailstones and fiery coals.

14 Hashem thundered from the heavens, and the Supreme God resounded with hailstones and fiery coals.

15 He sent His arrows and scattered them; with a barrage of lightning bolts, He terrified them.

16 And the depths of the sea became visible, and the pillars of the earth were revealed, from Your rebuke, Hashem, from the blast of breath that came from Your nostrils.

PSALM EIGHTEEN

17 He sent from on high and took me; He saved me from turbulent waters.

18 He saved me from my mighty enemies and from those who hate me, for they are stronger than me.

19 They confronted me on the day of my troubles, but Hashem was my support.

20 He brought me out to a place of expanse; He rescued me because He delighted in me.

21 Hashem recompenses me in accordance with my righteousness; He answers me according to the unblemished deeds of my hands.

22 For I have observed the ways of Hashem and have not veered in the way of evil from my God.

23 For all His statutes are before my eyes and I will not sever myself from His laws.

24 I will be unblemished with Him, for I will guard myself from wickedness.

25 Hashem will repay me according to my righteous deeds; the unblemished deeds of my hands are evident to Him.

26 With the pious person, act in piety; with an innocent person, act innocently.

27 With the faithful person, act in good faith; with a crooked person, act perversely.

28 For You will save a downtrodden people, and You will humble those with haughty eyes.

29 For You will illuminate my candle; Hashem, my God, will brighten my darkness.

30 For with You, I can blitz a battalion; and with my God, I can leap over walls.

31 As for God, His way is perfect; Hashem's promise is untainted; He is a shield to all who take refuge in Him.

32 For who is God other than Hashem, and who is a Rock except for our God?

33 The God who fortifies me in strength and clears my path of obstacles.

34 He makes my legs swift like those of a deer and places me on my peak of potential.

35 He prepares my hands for battle and strengthens my arms like a bow of copper.

36 You have given me the shield of Your salvation; Your right hand sustains me, and You have treated me with abundant humility.

PSALM EIGHTEEN

37   You have broadened my stride, so my feet have not faltered.

38   I will pursue my enemies and overtake them; I will not return until they are eradicated.

39   I crushed them so they cannot get up; they have fallen under my feet.

40   You have strengthened me for battle; You have subdued those who rise against me under my feet.

41   You made my enemies retreat; I eliminated those who hate me.

42   They cried out to their idols, but there was no savior; they even cried to Hashem, but He didn't answer them.

43   I will pulverize them like dust in the wind; I'll discard them like sludge in the streets.

44   You have rescued me from the bickering of the people; You have placed me as the head of nations; even a people whom I don't know serve me.

45   As soon as they hear, they will obey me; foreigners who hate me, lie out of fear and say they love me.

46   Foreigners will wither; they will tremble from within their prison walls.

PSALM EIGHTEEN

47   Hashem lives! Blessed is my Rock! May the God of my salvation be glorified.

48   The God who grants me vengeance and Whose utterance has subdued nations under me.

49   He rescues me from my enemies; You uplift me from those who rise against me; rescue me from the man of violence.

50   Therefore, I will give thanks to You among the nations, Hashem, and I'll sing songs of praise to Your Name.

51   He magnifies the salvations of His king and does lovingkindness for His anointed one, for David and his offspring forever.

PSALM NINETEEN

The celestial bodies tell of Hashem's glory

1. For the conductor, a psalm by David:

2. The heavens declare God's glory and the sky tells of His handiwork.

3. Each day expresses praise, and each night heightens awareness of Hashem.

4. There is no utterance nor words of doubt; their voice is not heard.

5. Their alignment is apparent the world over, and their words reach the ends of the globe; in their midst, He has placed a tent for the sun.

6. And the sun rises every morning like a groom emerging from his wedding canopy, rejoicing like a powerful warrior running his course.

7. Its point of origin is one end of the heavens, and its cycle is to the other end; nothing is hidden from its heat.

PSALM NINETEEN

8 Hashem's Torah is unblemished, it restores the soul; Hashem's testimony is trustworthy, giving wisdom even to a fool.

9 Hashem's statutes are upright, gladdening the heart; Hashem's commandments are pure, enlightening the eyes.

10 The glory of Hashem is pure, lasting forever; the judgments of Hashem are true, altogether just.

11 They are more appealing than gold, finer than platinum, and sweeter than honey, even more than the nectar of honeycombs.

12 Truly, Your servant has carefully observed Your commandments, for there is great reward for keeping them.

13 Who can fully avoid unintentional transgressions? Cleanse me from any sin that I'm not aware of.

14 Also protect Your servant from intentional sins; do not let them rule over me, so I can be unblemished and cleansed of severe sin.

15 May the words of my mouth and the meditations of my heart be acceptable to You, Hashem, my Rock and my Redeemer.

PSALM TWENTY

An appeal to Hashem in times of trouble and emergency

1. For the conductor, a psalm by David:

2. May Hashem answer you on your day of distress, and may the Name of the God of Jacob uplift you.

3. May He send your help from the Holy Sanctuary; may He support you from Zion.

4. May He remember all your prayers and accept them forever like a sacrificial offering.

5. May He grant you all your heart's desires and fulfill all of your aspirations.

6. We will rejoice in Your salvation and raise our flag in the Name of God; may Hashem fulfill all of your requests.

7. Now I know that Hashem has rescued His anointed one; He will answer him from His holy heavens; His right hand is the might of salvation.

8. Some trust in chariots and some in horses, but we call out in the Name of Hashem our God.

PSALM TWENTY

9 They collapsed and fell, but we rose and stood firm.

10 Hashem, save us! The King will answer us on the day that we call.

PSALM TWENTY-ONE

The virtue of trusting in Hashem, and especially a national leader who trusts in Hashem

1   For the conductor, a psalm by David:

2   Hashem, the king rejoices in Your might and is overjoyed in Your salvation.

3   You have granted him his heart's wishes, and You have not denied the requests of his lips.

4   Even before he asked, You preceded him with blessings of goodness; You placed a crown of fine gold on his head.

5   He requested life from You; You gave him length of days and eternity.

6   Great is his glory by virtue of Your salvation; You bestow him with majesty and splendor.

7   You bestow blessings on him forever; You delight him with joy in Your presence.

8   For the king trusts in Hashem and Supreme compassion, so he will never falter.

PSALM TWENTY-ONE

9 The blow of Your hand will reach all Your enemies; Your right hand will find those who hate You.

10 You will make them a fiery furnace at the time of Your wrath; Hashem, in His anger, will swallow them up, and a fire will consume them.

11 You will eliminate their offspring from the earth and their progeny from humanity.

12 For they plotted evil against You; they contrived a scheme that they could not implement.

13 For You will splinter them and Your bowstring will be drawn against them.

14 Be exalted, Hashem, in Your might; we will sing and chant praise at Your power!

PSALM TWENTY-TWO[7]

The individual's prayer for redemption from the lengthy exile and its tribulations

1   For the conductor, at the crack of dawn, a psalm by David:

2   My God, my God, why have You abandoned me, so far from my salvation and the sound of my cries of anguish?

3   O my God, I call out by day, but You don't answer; by night, there is no rest for me either.

4   Yet You are the Holy One; the praises of Israel are Your throne.

5   Our fathers trusted in You; they trusted, and You rescued them.

6   They cried out to You and were saved; they trusted in You and were not disappointed.

---

7   This is the psalm that Esther recited after fasting for three days, as she risked her life by entering King Achashverosh's chambers without being invited (Megilla 15b).

7   I'm a worm and not a human; the object of people's scorn and mockery.

8   Everyone who sees me mocks me; they open their mouths and shake their heads.

9   Hashem rescues the person who trusts in Him; He saves him because He desires him.

10   For You took me from the womb and sustained me on my mother's breasts.

11   From the moment I was born, I cast my trust on You; from my mother's womb, You are my God.

12   Don't be far from me, for trouble is near and no one else can help.

13   Many kings surround me; the mighty, like the bulls of Bashan, besiege me.

14   They open their mouths to devour me like a roaring and ravaging lion.

15   I've been poured out like water, and all my bones are out of joint; my heart melts like wax within me.

16   My strength is dried up like clay in a kiln, and my tongue clings to my palate; You have cast me down in the dust of death.

PSALM TWENTY-TWO

17 For dogs have surrounded me; a throng of evildoers has encircled me, as if my hands and feet were lion's prey.

18 If I tell everything that's happening to me, they'll simply look at me and gloat.

19 They divide my clothes among themselves and cast lots to plunder everything I own.

20 But You, Hashem, don't be far away! You are my strength, come quickly to help me!

21 Rescue me from the sword, my soul from vicious enemies.

22 Save me from the mouth of the lion and answer my plea for rescue from the horns of wild oxen.

23 I will tell of Your Name to my brothers, and I will praise You from the midst of the congregation.

24 You that revere Hashem, praise Him! All you offspring of Jacob, honor Him! All you offspring of Israel, fear Him!

25 For He has neither scorned nor loathed the cry of the poor person and has not hidden His face from him and will hear his call to Him.

26 My praising You among the multitudes comes from Your salvation; I will fulfill my vows in the presence of those who fear Him.

27 The humble will eat and be satiated; those who seek Hashem will praise Him – may your hearts live forever.

28 Those from the far ends of the earth will remember and return to Hashem; all the families of mankind will bow down before You.

29 For the kingdom is Hashem's; He rules over all the nations.

30 Every righteous person will share in the prosperity of the land, eat and bow down to Him; the wicked person who descends to the grave will kneel before Him, but his soul will not be revived.

31 The wonders that God performed for those who served Him will be told to future generations.

32 They will come and tell the next generation all that He has done.

PSALM TWENTY-THREE

Unconditional trust in Hashem

1. A Psalm by David: Hashem is my shepherd; I will not lack.

2. He gives me peacefulness in lush pastures; He leads me beside the calming waters.

3. He restores my soul and leads me along the paths of righteousness for His Name's sake.

4. Although I walk in the valley of death's shadow, I will not fear, for You are with me; Your rod and Your staff –they comfort me.

5. You have set a table before me in view of my enemies; You anointed my head with oil, my cup overflows.

6. May only goodness and lovingkindness pursue me all the days of my life, and may I dwell in the house of Hashem forever.

PSALM TWENTY-FOUR

The righteous of heart merit Hashem's blessings

1. A psalm by David: the Land of Israel and all it contains; the entire world and all its inhabitants belong to Hashem.

2. For He built its foundations on the seas and set it firmly on the rivers.

3. Who may ascend Hashem's mountain and who may stand in His holy place?

4. A person with clean hands and a pure heart; one who has not taken My Name in vain or sworn deceitfully.

5. He will receive Hashem's blessing and generosity from the God of his salvation.

6. This is the generation of those who seek Him, who yearn for Your Presence, the nation of Jacob, forever.

7. Holy gates, lift up your heads! Eternal doors, stand erect so that the King of Glory may enter.

8. Who is the King of Glory? Hashem, the strong and mighty, Hashem, the hero of battle.

PSALM TWENTY-FOUR

9   Holy gates, raise your heads! Eternal doors, open wide so that the King of Glory may enter.

10 Who is the King of Glory? Hashem, the Lord of Legions, He is the King of Glory forever.

PSALM TWENTY-FIVE

The individual who trusts exclusively in Hashem is the one who is worthy of salvation

1. By David: I lift up my soul to You, Hashem.

2. My God, I trust in You; therefore, I will not be shamed; do not let my enemies rejoice over me.

3. Don't let those who hope in You be shamed; let those who act treacherously without reason be ashamed.

4. Show me Your ways, Hashem; teach me Your paths.

5. Guide me in Your truth and teach me that You are the God of my salvation; I put my hope in You all day long.

6. Remember Your mercy and lovingkindness, Hashem, for they are eternal.

7. Don't remember the sins of my youth and my misdeeds; remember my deeds that are worthy of Your compassion, for the sake of Your goodness, Hashem.

8. Hashem is good and righteous; therefore, He will teach sinners the way.

PSALM TWENTY-FIVE

9   He guides the humble in justice and teaches the humble His way.

10   The ways of Hashem are all truth and compassion for those who uphold His covenant and His laws.

11   For Your Name's sake, Hashem, forgive my sin, for it is immense.

12   Hashem will teach any person who reveres Him the path that he should choose.

13   His soul will rest in goodness and his offspring will inherit the land.

14   Hashem reveals His secret to those who revere Him and informs them of His covenant.

15   My eyes always seek Hashem, for He will free my feet from the snare.

16   Turn to me and pardon me, for I am alone and afflicted.

17   The troubles of my heart have spread; bring me out of my sufferings.

18   See my affliction and my pain and forgive all my sins.

19   See my enemies, for they have become numerous; they hate me with fierce cruelty.

PSALM TWENTY-FIVE

20 Guard my soul and rescue me; don't let me suffer shame, for I take refuge in You.

21 Let innocence and integrity protect me, for I hope in You.

22 God, redeem Israel from all its troubles.

PSALM TWENTY-SIX

The righteous individual walks the path of innocence; therefore, Hashem will surely rescue him from those who hate him

1. By David: judge me, Hashem, for I have walked in my integrity, and I have trusted in Hashem; I will not stumble.

2. Examine me, Hashem, and test me; scrutinize my heart and my innermost thoughts.

3. For I am constantly mindful of Your lovingkindness and I have walked in Your true path.

4. I did not associate with unscrupulous people, nor did I come into contact with hypocrites.

5. I despised the clique of evildoers and refused to mingle with the wicked.

6. I wash my hands to cleanse them of sin so I can encircle Your altar, Hashem.

7. I will amplify the voice of gratitude and tell of all Your wondrous deeds.

PSALM TWENTY-SIX

8   Hashem, I love the abode of Your Sanctuary and the place of Your glorious Tabernacle.

9   Don't put my soul in the company of sinners, nor my life with men of bloodshed;

10   whose hands are full of conspiracy, whose right hands overflow with bribery.

11   As for me, I will walk in my integrity; redeem me and be gracious with me.

12   My foot stands on the straight path; in huge gatherings, I will bless Hashem.

PSALM TWENTY-SEVEN

A request for the ultimate good – closeness to Hashem

1. By David: Hashem is my light and my salvation; whom must I fear? Hashem is my life's strength; whom should I be afraid of?

2. When evildoers come near me to devour my flesh, my oppressors and my enemies, they are the ones who stumble and fall.

3. If an army besieges me, my heart will not fear; if war breaks out against me, in this I trust.

4. I have one request of Hashem that I seek constantly; may I dwell in the House of Hashem all the days of my life; to behold the beauty of Hashem and to frequent His Sanctuary.

5. For He will hide me in His shelter on the day of evil; He conceals me in the hidden place of His tent and uplifts me upon a rock.

6. Now my head will be raised above my enemies around me, and I will offer sacrifices with joyous song in His Tabernacle; I will sing songs of praise to Hashem.

PSALM TWENTY-SEVEN

7   Hashem, hear my voice when I call; be gracious to me and answer me.

8   My heart says in Your behalf, "Seek His Presence." I seek Your Presence, Hashem.

9   Don't hide Your face from me; don't reject Your servant in anger. You have always been my help; do not forsake me, do not abandon me, God of my salvation.

10 Even though my father and my mother have abandoned me, Hashem takes care of me.

11 Teach me Your way, Hashem; lead me along the upright path, so that my ever-vigilant enemies won't rejoice.

12 Don't hand me over to the will of my oppressors, for false witnesses have risen against me who spew violence.

13 Had I not believed that I would see Hashem's goodness in the land of the living...

14 Hope in Hashem; be strong and fortify your heart and hope in Hashem.

PSALM TWENTY-EIGHT

A prayer to avoid contact with evil people

1. By David: I call out to You, Hashem; don't turn a deaf ear to me, for if You don't answer my prayer, I'll be like those who descend into an abyss.

2. Hear the voice of my prayer as I cry out to You with outstretched hands from Your Holy Sanctuary.

3. Do not place me in the company of the wicked, with the sinful who speak peace with their companions but harbor evil in their hearts.

4. Give them what they deserve in accordance with the evil of their schemes; let them be repaid for their actions and recompensed in kind.

5. For they do not regard Hashem's deeds or the work of His hands; may He tear them down and not build them back up.

6. Blessed is Hashem, for He has heard the voice of my prayers.

7. Hashem is my strength and my shield; my heart trusted in Him, and I was helped; my heart rejoices, and I will thank Him in song.

PSALM TWENTY-EIGHT

8 Hashem is strength to those who depend on Him, and He is a stronghold of salvation for His anointed.

9 Save Your nation and bless Your inheritance; tend to them and uplift them forever.

PSALM TWENTY-NINE

A call to sanctify Hashem's Name around the world

1. A psalm by David: give tribute to Hashem, you sons of greatness; give tribute to Hashem with honor and strength.

2. Give tribute to Hashem in honor of His Name; bow down to Hashem in the splendor of holiness.

3. Hashem's voice is upon the waters; the God of Glory thunders; Hashem's voice is upon vast waters.

4. The voice of Hashem is powerful; the voice of Hashem is majestic.

5. The voice of Hashem fells cedars; Hashem shatters the cedars of Lebanon.

6. He makes them prance like a young calf, Mount Lebanon and Mount Hermon like antelopes.

7. The voice of Hashem hurls flames of fire.

8. The voice of Hashem makes the desert shudder; Hashem makes the desert of Kadesh shudder.

PSALM TWENTY-NINE

9   The voice of Hashem terrifies the mighty and strips the forests bare, and everything in His Temple speaks of His glory.

10 During the flood, Hashem sat on His throne; Hashem will be enthroned as King forever.

11 Hashem gives courage to His nation; Hashem will bless His nation with peace.

PSALM THIRTY

Just as the deepest darkness precedes the dawn, tribulations come before lasting success

1   David's psalm, the song that he composed for the dedication of the Holy Temple.

2   I will praise You, Hashem, for You have elevated me and have not let my enemies rejoice over me.

3   Hashem, my God, I cried out to You and You healed me.

4   Hashem, You uplifted my soul from the depths of the grave and have saved me from descending into an abyss.

5   Sing praise to Hashem, His fervent followers, and give thanks when invoking His Holy Name.

6   For His anger is momentary, but His favor lasts a lifetime; in the evening, one goes to bed in tears, but in the morning, one rises in joy.

7   During my time of tranquility, I thought that I'd never falter.

PSALM THIRTY

8   Hashem, by Your will, You lifted me to the heights of greatness, but when You hid Your face, I shuddered in fear.

9   I will call to You, Hashem, and appeal to the Lord.

10 What's the benefit of my descending to the grave? Will the dust thank You? Will it proclaim Your truth?

11 Hear my voice, Hashem, and be gracious with me; Hashem, help me!

12 You transformed my lamentation into dancing; You removed my mourning garment and dressed me in joy.

13 So that my soul will sing praise to You and not be silent; Hashem, my God, I will thank You forever.

PSALM THIRTY-ONE

Steadfast trust in Hashem despite tribulations and persecution

1. For the conductor, a psalm by David:

2. I have taken refuge in You, Hashem; may I never be ashamed. By virtue of Your benevolence, deliver me!

3. Hear my plea and rescue me quickly! Be a rock-solid stronghold for me, a mighty fortress to save me.

4. For You are my rock and my fortress; guide me and lead me for the sake of Your Name.

5. Take me out of this trap that they have set for me for You are my stronghold.

6. I entrust my spirit in Your hand; You have redeemed me, Hashem, God of truth.

7. I despise those who cling to empty idols; but as for me, I put my trust in Hashem.

8. I will rejoice in Your lovingkindness, for You have seen my affliction; You have known the troubles of my soul.

9. You did not hand me over to the enemy; You have set my feet in an expansive place.

PSALM THIRTY-ONE

10 Be gracious with me, Hashem, for I am in distress; my eyes waste away with grief, as well as my soul and my body.

11 For my life is ending in misery and my years in sorrow; my strength diminishes because of my sins and my bones are wasting away.

12 I have become a disgrace from so many tormentors, and especially among my neighbors, a scare to those who know me; people who see my outside run away from me.

13 I am forgotten like a dead person erased from people's hearts; I have become like some discarded utensil.

14 For I have heard many people's defamations, terrorizing me from all sides while conspiring against me and plotting to take my soul.

15 But I have trusted in You, Hashem; I always say that You are my God.

16 Every moment of my life is in Your hand; rescue me from the grasp of my enemies and pursuers.

17 May Your face shine on Your servant and in Your lovingkindness, save me!

PSALM THIRTY-ONE

18 Hashem, don't let me be shamed, for I call out to You; let the evil people be shamed and be silenced to the grave.

19 May lying lips become mute, the ones that talk in arrogance and contempt about the righteous.

20 How great is the goodness that You set aside for those who revere You, the goodness that You have performed for those who trust in You, for all people to see.

21 Hide them under cover of Your face from bands of evil people; conceal them in Your shelter from malicious tongues.

22 Blessed is Hashem, for He has been amazingly kind to me in the besieged city.

23 And I said in haste that You abandoned me; but really, You heard the voice of my prayers when I cried out to You.

24 Love Hashem, all of you who are devoted to Him! Hashem protects all who believe in Him, but repays the arrogant who act in conceit.

25 Be strong and courageous of heart, all who yearn for Hashem.

PSALM THIRTY-TWO

Fortunate is the individual who repents in earnest

1. By David, retold in contemporary language by a wise orator: happy is the person whose transgressions are forgiven and whose sins are obscured.

2. Happy is the person to whom Hashem does not attribute wickedness, for in his spirit there is no duplicity.

3. If I had failed to repent, my bones would have deteriorated from my roaring in anguish all day long.

4. For day and night, Your hand is heavily upon me; my strength evaporated like a drought in an everlasting summer.

5. Therefore, I admitted my sin to You and have not concealed my wickedness; I said that I'll confess my transgressions to Hashem, and You have forgiven the wickedness of my sin forever.

6. For this, any devout person should pray at an auspicious time that a rushing tidal wave should not subdue him.

PSALM THIRTY-TWO

7. You are a shelter for me; You protect me from distress; You envelop me with jubilant songs of deliverance forever.

8. "I shall enlighten you and illuminate the path that you should take; I shall advise you, for My eye is watching over you."

9. Don't be like a senseless horse or mule; their mouths must be restrained with a bit and bridle, so they don't come near you and bite.

10. The wicked suffer many agonies, but lovingkindness surrounds the person who trusts in Hashem.

11. Rejoice in Hashem and be glad, you righteous people; let all the upright of heart sing for joy.

PSALM THIRTY-THREE

Hashem's Divine Direction of everything in the universe brings joy to the righteous

1. Righteous people, sing joyfully to Hashem! It is befitting for the upright to praise Him.

2. Thank Him with the lyre; sing praise to Him with a ten-stringed harp.

3. Sing Him a new song; play adeptly with the sound of jubilance.

4. For the word of Hashem is upright; His every deed is done in complete faith.

5. He loves righteousness and justice; Hashem's lovingkindness fills the earth.

6. The heavens were made by Hashem's word; the heavenly legions by the breath of His mouth.

7. He gathers the waters of the sea and holds back the powerful oceans, so they won't flood the earth.

8. Let all the earth revere Hashem; may all the globe's inhabitants revere Him.

PSALM THIRTY-THREE

9   For He spoke, and it came to be; He commanded, and it stood forever.

10   Hashem nullifies the schemes of the nations; He thwarts the evil designs of the peoples.

11   Hashem's plan endures forever; what He designs lasts from generation to generation.

12   Happy is the nation whose God is Hashem; the people He chose to be His own.

13   Hashem looks down from heaven and sees all of humanity.

14   From His abode in heaven, He oversees all the inhabitants of the earth.

15   He Who forms the hearts of all, Who understands all of their doings.

16   A king's massive army doesn't guarantee victory, nor does a mighty warrior's power save him in battle.

17   The horse is a false hope for salvation; despite its great strength, it won't save its rider.

18   Hashem watches over all those who revere Him, all those who yearn for His lovingkindness;

PSALM THIRTY-THREE

19   to save their soul from death and to sustain them in famine.

20   Our souls wait in hope for Hashem; He is our help and our shield.

21   Our hearts rejoice in Him, for we have trusted in His Holy Name.

22   May Your lovingkindness be upon us, Hashem, just as we have longed for You.

PSALM THIRTY-FOUR

Trust in Hashem is a catalyst for salvation and miracles

1. By David, when he feigned insanity in front of Avimelech who chased him away and he went.[8]

2. I will bless Hashem at all times; His praise is always in my mouth.

3. My soul shall glorify Hashem; let the humble hear and rejoice.

4. Declare Hashem's greatness with me and let us praise His Name together.

5. I sought Hashem and He answered me; He saved me from everything I was afraid of.

---

8   This psalm refers to I Samuel, Chapter 21; David, in fleeing from King Saul and his troops, crossed the border into hostile Philistine, was taken captive and incarcerated in the castle dungeon of King Achish (aka Avimelech). To save himself, David feigned insanity. King Achish, who had an insane daughter, could not stand the additional yelling and shrieking of the deranged prisoner, whom he didn't believe was David, and chased him away. Freed, David thanks and praises Hashem.

6   Those who looked to Him became radiant; their faces will never be downcast.

7   When this poor man calls out, Hashem hears and saves him from all his troubles.

8   An angel of Hashem camps around those who revere Him and rescues them.

9   Taste and see how good Hashem is; happy is the man who takes refuge in Him.

10   Fear Hashem, His holy ones, for those who revere Him lack nothing.

11   Young lions may grow weak and hungry, but those who seek Hashem will not lack abundance.

12   Come, my sons, listen to me, and I will teach you what it means to fear Hashem.

13   Who is the man who desires life, who loves days of seeing good?

14   Guard your tongue from evil and your lips from speaking deceit.

15   Turn from evil and do good; seek peace and pursue it.

16   Hashem's eyes look toward the righteous, and His ears are attentive to their prayers.

PSALM THIRTY-FOUR

17 Hashem casts His face against evildoers, to erase their memory from the earth.

18 The righteous cried out, and Hashem heard and rescued them from all their troubles.

19 Hashem is close to the brokenhearted and saves those with crushed spirits.

20 Even though the troubles of the righteous person might be many, Hashem will rescue him from all of them.

21 Hashem guards all his bones; not a single one of them was broken.

22 Evil will slay the wicked, and those who hate the righteous person will be condemned.

23 Hashem redeems the souls of His servants, and all those who trust in Him will have no regret.

PSALM THIRTY-FIVE

A prayer for deliverance from oppressors

1. By David: Hashem, fight my enemies; battle those who battle against me.

2. Grab a shield and armor and rise up to help me.

3. Draw Your spear and block my pursuers; tell my soul, "I am your deliverance."

4. Let those who seek my life be shamed and humiliated; may those who plot against me retreat in disgrace.

5. May they be like chaff in the wind and may Hashem's angel repel them.

6. Let their way be dark and slippery, with Hashem's angel pursuing them.

7. For no reason, they laid a trap for me to fall into their net; for no cause, they dug a pit to kill me.

8. Let disaster come upon each of them unexpectedly; may they be caught in their own hidden trap and fall into it in disaster.

PSALM THIRTY-FIVE

9   Then my soul will rejoice in Hashem and rejoice in His salvation.

10   All my bones will say, "Hashem, who is like You? You save the poor person from someone stronger than him, the poor and the destitute from one that would rob them."

11   Malicious witnesses rise up to interrogate me about things that I have no knowledge of.

12   They repay me evil for good, seeking death for my soul.

13   Yet when they were sick, I wore sackcloth; I tortured myself with fasting; may the prayer that I prayed for them manifest in me.

14   As if they were my friend or brother, I walked around like someone in mourning for his mother, bent over in gloom.

15   When I limped, they rejoiced and gathered; even the wretched gathered against me; they tore at my flesh and would not be silenced.

16   For the sake of a cheap meal, they'd flatter the agitators and ridicule me, gritting their teeth at me.

PSALM THIRTY-FIVE

17 Lord, how long will You look on? Rescue my soul from their disastrous designs, my very essence from the young lions.

18 I will thank You in a massive congregation; I will praise You in a large gathering of people.

19 Don't let my treacherous enemies rejoice in my downfall; those who hate me for no reason wink their eyes in mockery.

20 They don't speak peace, yet they scheme in deceit against the downtrodden of the earth.

21 They open their mouth wide against me and say, "Aha, Aha, we have seen his downfall."

22 Hashem, You saw their glee – don't be silent! Lord, don't be far from me.

23 Awaken and arouse Your heavenly court to judge my case; my God and my Lord, rally to my cause.

24 Judge me in accordance with Your righteousness, Hashem, my God, and don't let them rejoice over me.

25 Don't let them think, "Aha, we got what we wanted." Don't let them say, "We have swallowed him."

PSALM THIRTY-FIVE

26   May all those who rejoice in my misfortune be disgraced and subdued together; may all those who look down on me be clad in shame and disgrace.

27   May those who desire my vindication sing and rejoice; let them always say, "Be gloried, Hashem, Who desires the well-being of His servant."

28   Then my tongue will express Your righteousness and praise You all day long.

PSALM THIRTY-SIX

The wicked pursue sins but the righteous take refuge in Hashem's light

1. For the conductor, by the servant of Hashem, by David:

2. I imagine in my heart how the evil inclination tells the wicked person that he need not fear God.

3. The evil inclination beautifies transgression in the eyes of the evil person, so that Hashem should find his wickedness and hate it.

4. The words of his mouth are wickedness and deceit; he no longer has the sense to do good.

5. He devises deceit while lying in bed; he positions himself on a path that is not good, and he does not disdain evil.

6. Hashem, Your lovingkindness is in the heavens, Your faithfulness reaches the skies.

7. Your righteousness is like the mighty mountains; Your judgments are as unfathomable as the depths of the ocean; You save both man and animal, Hashem.

PSALM THIRTY-SIX

8   How precious is Your lovingkindness, Hashem! Mankind takes refuge in the shadow of Your wings.

9   They will be satiated from the abundance of Your house; You will let them drink of the stream that flows from Eden.

10   For You are the source of life; only in Your light do we see light.

11   Bestow Your kindness to those who know You, and Your charity to the upright of heart.

12   Let not the foot of the arrogant come near me, nor the hand of the wicked drive me away.

13   There, the spreaders of treachery fell, struck down, and unable to rise again.

PSALM THIRTY-SEVEN

The imminent downfall of the wicked and the eternal salvation that awaits the righteous

1 By David: do not compete with evildoers and do not be jealous of those who act unjustly.

2 For they will be mowed down like grass in the pasture and wither like green vegetation.

3 Trust in Hashem and do good; dwell in the land and live in faith.

4 And delight in Hashem and He will grant you your heart's wishes.

5 Turn to Hashem for all your needs; trust in Him, and He will act.

6 He will make your righteousness shine brightly and your just ways shine like the midday sun.

7 Be silent and wait in yearning for Hashem; don't compete with the person on a path of apparent success, the conniving individual.

8 Abstain from anger and wrath; don't compete with evildoers, for it only brings harm.

PSALM THIRTY-SEVEN

9 For the evildoers will be destroyed, but those who hope in Hashem shall inherit the land.

10 Shortly, the wicked person will disappear; look where he used to be, and he's no longer there.

11 And the humble will inherit the earth, delighting in an abundance of peace.

12 The wicked person plots against the righteous and grits his teeth at him.

13 The Lord laughs at him, for He sees that his day is coming.

14 The wicked wielded their swords and drew their bows, to bring down the poor and the destitute, and to slaughter upright people.

15 Their swords will pierce their own hearts, and the bows will be broken.

16 Better is the righteous person's tiny following than the many who align with the wicked.

17 For the arms of the wicked will be broken, but Hashem upholds the righteous.

18 Hashem knows the days of the flawless; their inheritance will be forever.

PSALM THIRTY-SEVEN

19 They won't grieve in times of disaster, and they'll be satiated in times of famine.

20 The wicked will perish and Hashem's enemies will dissipate like the morning mist in the valley, dispersed like smoke.

21 The wicked person borrows but does not repay, while the righteous person is compassionate and giving.

22 For the ones He blesses will inherit the land, but His accursed will be destroyed.

23 A devout man's stable footsteps are from Hashem, and He desires his way.

24 Even though he stumbles, he will not fall because Hashem holds him up.

25 I was young and now I am old, but I've never seen a righteous person forsaken nor his offspring begging for bread.

26 He is always compassionate and giving, and his offspring are a blessing.

27 Shun evil and do good, and you will stand forever.

28 For Hashem loves justice and will not forsake His pious people; they will be protected forever, but the offspring of the wicked will perish.

PSALM THIRTY-SEVEN

29   The righteous will inherit the land and abide forever upon it.

30   The mouth of the righteous individual expresses wisdom, and his tongue speaks justice.

31   With the Torah of his God in his heart, his feet will not falter.

32   The wicked person watches the righteous person and seeks to kill him.

33   Hashem will not abandon him to the hand of the wicked and will not let him be condemned when he is judged.

34   Cast your hope to Hashem and safeguard His way, and He will uplift you to inherit the land and you will see the destruction of the wicked.

35   I have seen a wicked tyrant, thriving like a robust native tree.

36   Yet he suddenly vanished and was gone; I sought him, but he was nowhere to be found.

37   Keep your eye on the man of integrity and look at the upright person, for the future of such an individual is peace.

38 Criminals will be destroyed together; the future of the wicked is ruin.

39 But the salvation of the righteous comes from Hashem, their stronghold in time of trouble.

40 Hashem will help them and rescue them; He rescues them from the wicked and saves them, for they trusted in Him.

PSALM THIRTY-EIGHT

From the depths of tribulations, a prayer for salvation

1. A psalm by David, as a reminder to those suffering tribulations:

2. Hashem, do not rebuke me in Your anger nor punish me in Your wrath.

3. For Your arrows have pierced me and Your hand has struck me.

4. All my flesh is wounded because of Your fury and there's no peace in my bones because of my sin.

5. For my sins have overwhelmed me; like a heavy burden, they are more than I can bear.

6. My wounds smell and fester because of my folly.

7. I am contorted and completely bent over; I walk around all day in gloom.

8. In my thoughts, I am full of disgrace, and my body is inflamed.

9. I am faint and exceedingly crushed; I roared from the groaning of my heart.

PSALM THIRTY-EIGHT

10 Lord, You are well aware of all my desires; my cries of pain are not hidden from You.

11 My heart is engulfed in sorrow; my strength has left me, and the light of my eyes has dimmed.

12 My friends and companions stand indifferent to my suffering, and my relatives stand far away.

13 Those who want to kill me set traps; those who want to harm me talk maliciously, and they speak deceit all day long.

14 I act like a deaf person who does not hear, like a mute who does not open his mouth.

15 I became like someone who does not hear and has no reply in his mouth.

16 For I look to You, Hashem; You will answer them, O Lord, my God.

17 For I fear that they will rejoice in my downfall; if I'd falter, they'd become even more inflated with arrogance.

18 For I am on the brink of collapse, and my pain is constant.

19 For I confess my sin and worry about my guilt.

PSALM THIRTY-EIGHT

20 My enemies live in abundance, and those who hate me become great through treachery.

21 And those who repay evil for good harass me for pursuing good.

22 Don't forsake me, Hashem; my God, don't be far from me.

23 Come quickly to help me, O Lord, my salvation.

PSALM THIRTY-NINE

Instead of questioning Hashem, one should accept everything with love

1. For the Conductor, for Yeduthun,[9] a psalm by David:

2. I resolved to guard myself so I would not sin with my tongue; I muzzle my mouth even when an evil person stands before me and torments me.

3. I became silent like a mute, not even saying a word of prayer or Torah, and so my pain intensified.

4. My heart burned within me, and my thoughts were ablaze, so I had to speak out to You.

5. Let me know when my end is, Hashem, and the measure of my days, so I'll know when my suffering will end.

6. You have made my days as if they were measured in inches; my lifespan is like nothing before You; all of human existence is fleeting in vanity, forever.

---

9 One of the Levite singers in the Holy Temple who was particularly designated to sing this psalm

PSALM THIRTY-NINE

7   Only a man walks around in darkness but pursues his lusts in vain; he amasses wealth but doesn't know whom he's gathering it for.

8   And now, what do I hope for, O Lord? I put my hope in You.

9   Save me from my transgressions; don't let me become the mockery of fools.

10 I became mute and didn't open my mouth, because it is You Who has done everything.

11 Remove Your plague from me; I am devastated from the fear of Your hands' blows.

12 While rebuking wickedness, You chastise a person and consume his health like a moth eating cloth; all mankind is nothing but futility, forever.

13 Hear my prayers, Hashem, and listen to my outcry; don't ignore my tears for I am a wayfarer with You in this world, a temporary resident like my forefathers.

14 Remove your punishment from me and allow me to get stronger before I am no more.

PSALM FORTY

Fortunate is the person who trusts in Hashem and does His will

1. For the conductor, a psalm by David:

2. I have forever hoped in Hashem; He was attentive to me, and He heard my prayer.

3. He lifted me out of the pit of turmoil, from muck and mud; He set my feet on solid ground and steadied my stride.

4. He put a new song in my mouth, praise to our God; many will see and stand in awe, and they will trust in Hashem.

5. Happy is the man who has placed his trust in Hashem, neither turning to the arrogant or those who follow falsehood.

6. Many are the marvelous deeds that You have done, Hashem my God; all Your wonders and thoughts on our behalf – nothing can compare to You; it is too much to recount.

7. You did not desire sacrifices and meal offerings; You opened my ears to obey You; neither burnt offerings nor sin offerings did You request.

PSALM FORTY

8   Then I said, "Look, I have come with a scroll of a book that is written about me."

9   My desire is to do Your will, my God; Your Torah has become part of my soul.

10 I proclaimed Your righteousness in front of a large congregation; see, I will not restrain my lips; Hashem, You know this.

11 I did not hide Your benevolence as a secret in my heart; I spoke of Your faithfulness and Your salvation in public; I did not fail to publicize Your lovingkindness and Your truth in front of a massive audience.

12 You, Hashem, will not withhold Your mercy from me; Your compassion and Your truth always protect me.

13 For countless misfortunes have enveloped me; the punishments from so many sins have caught up with me that I can't see; they are more numerous than the hairs of my head, and my courage has abandoned me.

14 May it be Your will, Hashem, to rescue me; Hashem, come quickly to help me.

15 May those who seek to destroy my life be shamed and disgraced; may those who seek to harm me retreat in humiliation.

PSALM FORTY

16 Let them be appalled when disgrace comes back to them, those who ridiculed me and rejoiced in my troubles.

17 May those who seek You be happy and rejoice in You; may those who love Your salvation always say, "May Hashem be praised."

18 As for me, I am poor and destitute; my Lord, consider my submission to You favorably, for You are my help and my rescue; my God, do not delay.

PSALM FORTY-ONE

A prayer for healing and for rescue from enemies

1. For the conductor, a psalm by David:

2. Happy is the person who knows how to help the needy; Hashem will protect him on the day of evil.

3. Hashem will guard and revive him, and he will be happy on earth; He will not hand him over to the will of his enemies.

4. Hashem will come to his aid on his sickbed, even during heavy illness when he has no respite.

5. I said, "Hashem, be gracious to me; heal my soul for I have sinned against You."

6. My enemies speak maliciously about me, "When will he die, and his name be obliterated?"

7. And if one of them visits, he speaks in false sympathy while harboring evil in his heart; once he goes outside, he spreads the evil around.

8. Together, all those who despise me whisper about me; they conjure my harm.

PSALM FORTY-ONE

9. They curse me, "His transgression clings to him; now that he is bedridden, he shall not get up again."

10. Even my ally, whom I trusted, and who ate my bread, lies in ambush to trap me.

11. And You, Hashem, be gracious to me and raise me up from sickness so I can repay them.

12. That way, I'll know that You desire me, when my enemy won't be able to shout in triumph over me.

13. By virtue of my integrity, You will hold me up and place me in Your presence forever.

14. Blessed is Hashem, the God of Israel, from eternity to eternity, amen and amen!

BOOK TWO

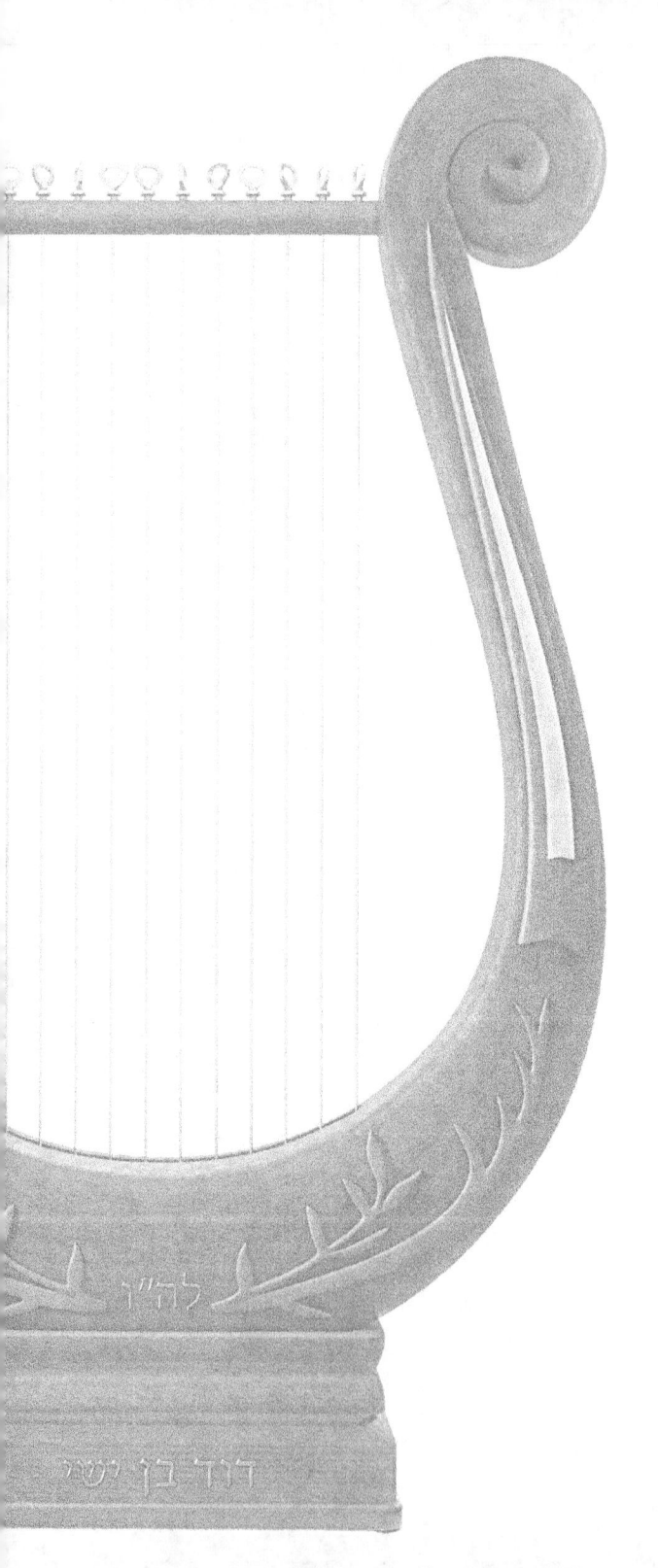

PSALM FORTY-TWO

The tremendous yearning for Hashem and the anticipation of salvation

1 For the conductor, by the sons of Korach, retold in contemporary language by a wise orator:

2 Like a deer that yearns for a stream, so does my soul yearn for You, O God.

3 My soul thirsts for God, for the living God; when will I ever come and appear before God?

4 For me, my tears have become my sustenance day and night, for my enemies taunt me all day long, "Where is your God?"

5 These things I remember as I pour out my soul, how I walked nobly with a throng of people to the House of God, with the joyous song and thanks among the many.

6 Why are you downcast, my soul? Why do you moan within me? Cast your hope to God, for I will yet thank Him for the salvation that comes from His presence.

7 My God, my soul is downcast, for I remember You from the land of Jordan, from the Hermon peaks and Mount Sinai.

PSALM FORTY-TWO

8   One deep trouble summons another, and calamity like the crash of a tidal wave's rushing waters has swept over me.

9   May Hashem command His lovingkindness in the day, and may I sing His praise at night; that is my prayer to the God of my life.

10   I will ask God, my Rock, "Why have You forgotten me? Why must I walk in darkness out of fear of the enemy?"

11   Like a murder weapon piercing my bones, my enemies taunt me all day long and say, "Where is your God?"

12   Why are you downcast, my soul? Why do you moan within me? Cast your hope to God, for I will yet thank Him for He is the light of my face and the God of my salvation.

PSALM FORTY-THREE

A prayer for rescue from enemies and to merit salvation

1. God, justify my cause and fight my battle against an unfaithful nation; rescue me from the deceitful and corrupt person.

2. For You are the God of my strength; why have You neglected me? Why must I walk around in darkness, oppressed by the enemy?

3. Send Your light and Your truth; they will guide me; they will bring me to Your holy mountain and to Your dwelling places.

4. And I will come to the altar of God, to God, the delight of my joy and thank You with the lyre, O God, my God.

5. Why are you downcast, my soul? Why do you moan within me? Cast your hope to God, for I will yet thank Him for He is the light of my face and the God of my salvation.

PSALM FORTY-FOUR

A prayer for the end of exile

1. For the conductor, composed by the sons of Korach, retold in contemporary language by a wise orator:

2. God, we have heard with our own ears, our fathers told us, the deeds that You performed in their days, in the days of old.

3. With Your hand, You drove out the nations from the Land of Israel and planted our forefathers in their place; you brought misfortune on the Canaanite nations and drove them away.

4. It was not by the sword nor strength of their arms that our forefathers took the land; it was Your right hand, Your arm and the light of Your face, because You favored them.

5. You are my King, O God; decree salvations for the House of Jacob.

6. With Your help, we can push back our oppressors; only by Your Name, can we subdue our enemies.

7. For I do not trust in my bow, nor does my sword rescue me.

PSALM FORTY-FOUR

8   Only You have saved us from our oppressors and brought shame on those who hate us.

9   We sang our praise of God all day long and will forever thank You, for eternity!

10   Even if You would abandon us and disgrace us and not accompany our armies.

11   Even though You make us retreat from the oppressor, when those who hate us plunder us at will.

12   You let them devour us like sheep and scatter us among the nations.

13   You sell your nation for nothing and no profit.

14   You make us a disgrace to our neighbors, the brunt of mockery and scorn to those around us.

15   You have made us a scapegoat among the nations, an object of derision among the peoples.

16   All day long, humiliation faces me; my face is covered in shame…

17   from the voice of the one who taunts and curses, from the vengeful enemy.

18   Despite all this, we have not forgotten You, nor have we denied Your covenant of Torah.

PSALM FORTY-FOUR

19   Our heart has not turned away from our belief in You, nor have our steps strayed from Your path...

20   even though You subdued us in the desert, the habitat of jackals and snakes, and enveloped us in the shadow of death.

21   Have we forgotten God's name and outstretched our hands to a strange god?

22   Surely God would have investigated this, for He knows the secrets of the heart.

23   For Your sake, we are killed all day long; we are regarded as sheep for slaughter.

24   Rise; why do You sleep, O Lord? Awaken and don't forsake us forever!

25   Why hide Your face – do You forget our affliction and oppression?

26   For our soul is face down in the dust; our belly clings to the earth.

27   Rise and come to our aid; redeem us for the sake of Your lovingkindness.

PSALM FORTY-FIVE

A song of endearment in praise of Torah scholars

1. For the conductor, composed by the sons of Korach, retold in contemporary language by a wise orator, a song of endearment in praise of Torah scholars:

2. My heart pulsates with beautiful words; I dedicate my sonnet to Torah scholars who resemble a king; my tongue is like the pen of a skillful scribe.

3. You are more beautiful than all of mankind; charm pours from your lips and therefore God has blessed you forever.

4. Buckle your sword upon your thigh to fight the war of Torah, for this is your splendor and your glory.

5. And your glory is that you will go forward in the cause of truth and righteous humility, and your students, your right hand, will do wondrous deeds.

6. Your arrows are sharp; nations will fall under you, for your arrows pierce the heart of the King's enemies.

7. You have the eternal throne of a judge and minister, for the scepter of justice and integrity is the scepter of your kingdom.

PSALM FORTY-FIVE

8 You have loved justice and have despised evil;
   therefore, God, your God, has anointed you with the
   oil of joy, more than your peers.

9 Myrrh, agarwood, and cassia are the fragrance of
   your clothes, even more than the ivory palaces, your
   reward from Me to please you.

10 The daughters of kings are your visitors; your
   wife stands erect at your right, adorned in the gold
   of Ophir.

11 Hear, O Congregation of Israel, and see the upright
   way; incline your ear to the words of Torah and forget
   the ways of the nations that influenced you and the
   idolatry of your ancient fathers.

12 If you do so, the King will desire your beautiful ways,
   for He is your Lord, and you must bow down to Him.

13 The wealthy people of Tyre will court your favor with
   lavish gifts.

14 The same Torah scholars whose honor was concealed
   are now clothed in gold-embroidered garments.

15 The nations will bring finely embroidered garments to
   the king of the land, and the peoples will follow Israel
   to join them, to come to You, Hashem.

PSALM FORTY-FIVE

16   They will be brought in joy and happiness to Zion, to come to the palace of the King.

17   Congregation of Israel, your sons will succeed your ancestors and will become leaders throughout the land.

18   I will proclaim Your Name in every generation; therefore, the nations will acknowledge You forever and ever.

PSALM FORTY-SIX

By virtue of trust in Hashem, there's nothing to fear

1. For the conductor, composed by the sons of Korach, a song to be played on the soprano instrument:

2. God is our refuge and source of strength, a help in distress, and very close by.

3. Therefore, we won't fear when the earth trembles and when mountains collapse into the deep seas.

4. Its waters rage and foam; the mountains quake from His glory, forever.

5. There is a river whose streams bring joy to the City of God, the holy dwelling place of the Almighty.

6. God is in its midst; it shall not fall. God will come to its aid at the dawn of the final redemption.

7. The nations will be in uproar and kingdoms will collapse; the earth will melt at the roar of His voice.

8. Hashem, the Master of Legions, is with us; the God of Jacob is a stronghold for us forever.

9 Go and see the deeds of Hashem; He has brought desolation on the nations.

10 He ends wars across the earth; He breaks the bow, shatters the spear, and burns chariots in fire.

11 "Desist and know that I am God! I shall be glorious among the nations; I shall be glorious on earth."

12 Hashem, the Master of Legions, is with us; the God of Jacob is a stronghold for us forever.

PSALM FORTY-SEVEN

Hashem reigns over the entire universe

1. For the conductor, composed by the sons of Korach, a psalm:

2. All you nations, join hands together; call out to God in euphoric song.

3. For Hashem is supreme, a prodigious King over all the earth.

4. He shall subdue nations under us and peoples under our feet.

5. He will choose our inheritance for us, the Holy Temple, the pride of Jacob that He loves forever.

6. Then God will ascend in ovation, in the blast of the shofar.

7. Sing praise to God, sing praise! Sing praise to our King, sing praise!

8. For God is King over all the earth; skilled musicians, play songs of praise!

PSALM FORTY-SEVEN

9 God reigns over all nations and sits on His holy throne.

10 The foremost people of the nations gathered together, the people of the God of Abraham, for the guardians of the earth belong to God; He is greatly praised.

PSALM FORTY-EIGHT

We shall rejoice in Hashem's salvation, and when the evil stand trial

1 A psalm composed by the sons of Korach:

2 Hashem is great and praiseworthy, in Jerusalem, His holy mountain, the city of our God.

3 Beautifully scenic, joy of the entire world, Mount Zion, on the north side of the great city of King David.

4 God in her palaces will be recognized as her Bastion of Strength.

5 The kings joined forces and advanced together.

6 At the sight of Hashem mobilizing against them, they were stunned; they fled in panic.

7 Trembling seized hold of them there like a woman in the height of labor pains.

8 Punish them with a strong east wind that demolishes the ships of Tarshish.

PSALM FORTY-EIGHT

9   Just as we heard from the prophets, we saw in the city of Hashem, the Master of Legions, the city of our God, may God establish it eternally, forever.

10   God, we hoped for Your compassion, to see salvation in the midst of Your sanctuary.

11   God, just as Your Name is great, so does Your praise reach the ends of the earth; benevolence fills Your right hand.

12   Let Mount Zion be happy, let all the towns of Judea rejoice, because of Your judgments.

13   Walk around Zion and circle her perimeter; count her towers.

14   Take note of her walls and traverse her palaces so that you can describe their beauty to the final generation.

15   For this is God, our God forever and ever; He will guide us forever.

PSALM FORTY-NINE

A warning to those who trust in material wealth and forget about their spiritual future

1. For the conductor, composed by the sons of Korach, a psalm:

2. Hear this, all the nations; listen up, all inhabitants of the world.

3. Sons of Abraham and sons of Noah alike, rich and poor together.

4. My mouth will speak wisdom, and my heart will provide insightful contemplations.

5. I will raise my ear to the words of Torah; I will begin my riddle for you with the lyre.

6. Why should I fear in days of evil? My own sins that I ignore will surround me on the day of judgment.

7. Those who rely on their material possessions and boast about their great wealth;

8. No one can bail out a brother to save him from death, nor can a person pay his ransom to God.

PSALM FORTY-NINE

9 People cannot redeem their souls with money, for that is eternally impossible.

10 Can a person live forever, never seeing the grave?

11 One can see that wise men die; the fool and the ignorant perish together and leave their wealth to others.

12 They imagine that their houses will stand forever, their dwellings from generation to generation; they memorialize their names in this world.

13 A man can't be sure that he'll wake up in the morning with his wealth; he resembles an animal that perishes.

14 This is their way of foolishness, and their offspring will continue to praise wealth like their fathers did.

15 Like sheep, they'll be herded into the grave, death will be their shepherd; and the upright will rule over them at the dawn of redemption; their bodies will rot in the grave, their eternal habitat.

16 But God will redeem my soul from the grasp of the grave, for He will take me on the upright path forever.

17 Don't envy the rich man when he amasses even more wealth.

PSALM FORTY-NINE

18 For when he dies, he takes nothing with him; his wealth will not accompany him to the grave.

19 Though he applauds his soul in his lifetime, everyone will praise you, the righteous person, because you improve yourself.

20 His soul will join the company of his ancestors; they will never see the light.

21 A man can't be sure that he'll wake up in the morning with his wealth; he resembles an animal that perishes.

PSALM FIFTY

Hashem isn't interested in ritual sacrifices; He desires one's sincere penitence

1. A psalm by Asaph; God, Hashem the Almighty, has spoken and summoned the earth from where the sun rises in the east to where it sets in the west.

2. From Zion, the epitome of beauty, He appeared.

3. Our God will arrive and He will not be silent; an all-consuming fire will precede Him, and extremely turbulent storms will surround Him.

4. He will summon the heavens above and the earth to avenge His people.

5. "Gather my devout ones unto Me, those who accepted My covenant, fulfilled the Torah, and engaged in prayer."

6. The heavens will proclaim His justice, for God is the Judge forever.

7. Hear, My people, and I will speak; and I bear witness against you, for I Am God. Your God.

PSALM FIFTY

8   I will not reprimand you for your lack of ritual sacrifices, nor are your burnt offerings My concern.

9   I do not need to take a bull from your estate or goats from your corrals.

10   For all the animals in the forest and the livestock grazing on thousands of mountain pastures are Mine.

11   I know every bird in the mountains and all the creatures in the fields are in My domain.

12   Even if I were hungry, I would ask nothing from you, for the world and all it contains is Mine.

13   Do I need to eat the flesh of bulls or drink the blood of goats?

14   The sacrifice I want is your confession to God and the fulfillment of your vows to the Almighty.

15   And when you call Me on a day of trouble, I will rescue you, and you will respect Me.

16   And God said to the evil person, "Why do you recite My laws and babble the words of My Torah with your mouth?"

17   And you're the one who despises rebuke and casts the words of My Torah by the wayside.

PSALM FIFTY

18   Whenever you saw a thief, you joined him, and you kept the company of adulterers.

19   Your mouth was the emissary of evil and your tongue clings to deceit.

20   You sit among people and talk against your brother; you slander the son of your mother.

21   You've done all this, but I have waited for you to repent; you thought that I condone your behavior; but now, I will reprimand you and itemize all your misdeeds for you to see.

22   Ponder this, those who are oblivious of God, for if I punish you, no one can rescue you.

23   An offering of confession honors Me; and to the person who follows the path of penitence, I will show the salvation of God.

PSALM FIFTY-ONE

Yearning for a pure heart and closeness to Hashem

1. For the conductor, a psalm by David:

2. When Nathan the Prophet came to chastise him for the incident of Batsheva.[10]

3. Forgive me, O God, as befits Your lovingkindness; in Your abundant mercy, erase my transgressions.

4. Cleanse me thoroughly of my wickedness and purify me of my sin.

5. For I admit my transgressions and am constantly aware of my sin.

6. I have sinned against You alone and I have done something that You detest; You are therefore justified in Your verdicts and fair in Your judgments.

7. Indeed, I was born through wickedness, and my mother conceived me in sin.

---

10 See II Samuel, Ch. 12

8. You desire that a person permeate himself with truth; infuse the hidden chambers of my heart with wisdom.

9. Purify me with hyssop as one would purify a leper, and I will be pure; cleanse me of sin until I am white as snow.

10. Let me hear the joy and happiness of forgiveness so the bones You purified may rejoice.

11. Hide Your face from my sins and erase all my sins.

12. O God, create a pure heart for me and renew within me an upright spirit.

13. Don't cast me away from You, and don't take Your holy spirit away from me.

14. Restore me the joy of Your salvation and instill a generous and willing spirit within me.

15. I will then teach Your ways to wrongdoers, and sinners will return to You.

16. Deliver me from the sentence of death, O Lord, God of my salvation, so that my tongue may sing of Your benevolence.

17. O Lord, open my lips so that my mouth can declare Your praise.

PSALM FIFTY-ONE

18 For You don't want an animal sacrifice from me, nor do You desire a burnt-offering.

19 The genuine sacrifices to God are a broken spirit; God does not reject a broken and humbled heart.

20 May You desire to favor Zion; rebuild the Holy Temple and the walls of Jerusalem.

21 Then, You will desire sacrifices offered in righteousness, burnt offerings and whole offerings; then, the priests will sacrifice young bulls on Your altar.

PSALM FIFTY-TWO

Those who slander others are cursed, while those who trust in Hashem are blessed

1. For the conductor, by David, retold in contemporary language by a wise orator:

2. When Doeg the Edomite came to inform Saul and told him, "David came to Ahimelech's house.[11]"

3. You, the self-proclaimed hero of Torah, why do you take pride in the evil you do? God's compassion is constant to save me from you.

4. Your tongue plots evil, like a sharp razor that cuts treacherously.

5. You loved evil more than good, always preferring the lie to righteous speech.

6. You loved all the words of devastation, the language of deceit.

---

11 See I Samuel, 22:9

PSALM FIFTY-TWO

7 Likewise, God will shatter you forever; He will sever and remove you from your tent and uproot you from the land of the living, forever.

8 The righteous will see and marvel in awe, and laugh at him:

9 "That's the man who did not take refuge in God; he trusted his vast wealth and took strength from his wickedness."

10 But I am like a thriving olive tree in the House of God; I trust in God's grace forever and ever.

11 I will thank You forever for what You have done, and I will yearn for Your Name, for it is good to those who are devoted to You.

PSALM FIFTY-THREE

The punishment that awaits the enemies of God and Israel, and the future salvation of Israel

1. For the conductor on the tambourine, by David, retold in contemporary language by a wise orator:

2. The decadent person said in his heart, "There is no God; corrupt people have acted despicably, and no one does good."

3. God gazes down from Heaven at mankind to see if there are any wise individuals who seek God.

4. All of them are impure; together, they have become depraved. There is no one who does good, not even one.

5. Don't those evildoers realize – the ones who devour my people like they eat bread, who do not call to God?

6. That they will be stricken with fear, an unprecedented fear; for God has scattered the bones of those who besiege you; you have put them to shame, for God has rejected them.

PSALM FIFTY-THREE

7 May the deliverance of Israel come from Zion; when God returns the captives of His people, Jacob will rejoice, Israel will rejoice.

PSALM FIFTY-FOUR

A prayer for deliverance from enemies

1 For the conductor of the orchestra, by David, retold in contemporary language by a wise orator:

2 When the people of Ziph came and informed Saul that David was hiding among them.[12]

3 O God, by Your Name, save me and by Your strength, take revenge for me.

4 O God, hear my prayer; listen to the words of my mouth.

5 For strangers have risen against me, and ruthless men want to kill me; they never think of God.

6 See, God is my helper; the Lord is the foundation of my soul.

7 He will repay the evil of those who look at me in evil; for the sake of Your truth, obliterate them.

---

12 See I Samuel, 23:19

PSALM FIFTY-FOUR

8   I will then sacrifice a voluntary offering to You; I will thank Your Name, Hashem, for it is good.

9   For He has rescued me from every trouble and has enabled me to see the downfall of my enemies.

PSALM FIFTY-FIVE

A prayer for salvation from enemies and for their downfall

1. For the conductor of the orchestra, by David, retold in contemporary language by a wise orator:

2. O God, listen to my prayer and don't ignore my plea.

3. Be attentive to me and answer me; I am upset;

4. from the clamor of the enemy, the wicked oppressor, for they accuse me of wrongdoing and hate me with a passion.

5. My heart trembles within me and the premonitions of death have befallen me.

6. I am afraid and trembling, and I am surrounded by horror.

7. And I said, "If only I had the wings of a dove! I would fly away and find a place of rest."

8. Surely, I would wander far away and find refuge in the wilderness forever.

PSALM FIFTY-FIVE

9   I would rush to find shelter from my enemies, who resemble a turbulent storm.

10   Devour them, O Lord, and render them speechless; for I have seen violence and strife in the city.

11   Day and night, the violence and strife make their rounds on the city's walls; injustice and falsehood are within.

12   Evil is in her midst; fraud and deceit never leave her streets.

13   For he is not a noticeable enemy that taunts me nor an adversary that threatens me, otherwise I would avoid him.

14   But you, an equal to me, a teacher and companion.

15   Together, we would share secrets of the Torah; we would walk together in the House of God.[13]

16   May He condemn them to death; may they suddenly descend to the grave, for evil dwells within them, in their hearts.

---

13 Verses 13-15 and 21-22 refer to King David's treacherous advisor Achitopel who betrayed him and supported Absalom's revolt (see II Samuel, Ch. 16). Verse 16 refers to Achitopel and his fellow conspirators.

PSALM FIFTY-FIVE

17 As for me, I will call to God and Hashem will save me.

18 Evening, morning, and noon, I pour out my heart in prayer, and He hears my voice.

19 He redeemed me unharmed from the battle against me, as if many were on my side.

20 God, the primordial Monarch, will hear and humble those who never consider their final day nor fear God.

21 He turned against his ally and broke his pact.

22 The words of his mouth were smoother than butter, yet his heart was at war; his expressions were more soothing than oil, yet they were really curses.

23 Cast your burden on Hashem and He will sustain you; He will not let the righteous falter.

24 And You, O God, lower them to the depths of the grave; murderous and treacherous men will not live half their days, but as for me, I will trust in You.

PSALM FIFTY-SIX

A prayer in times of trouble

1. For the conductor, a sonnet by David composed when he was like a silent dove far from home when the Philistines seized him in Gath:[14]

2. Have mercy on me, O God, for people want to swallow me alive; all day long, in belligerence, they oppress me.

3. They watch me all day long, yearning to eat me alive, for many are fighting against me, O Exalted One!

4. When I'm afraid, I trust in You.

5. In God, Whose attribute of judgment I praise, in God, I have trusted; I will not fear – what can mortals do to me?

6. Their constant torment makes me cry out in anguish; all their thoughts are malicious.

---

14 See I Samuel, 21:12

PSALM FIFTY-SIX

7   They gather together, lie in ambush and monitor my every step as they anticipate trapping me.

8   Do they deserve to escape the consequences of their wickedness? Subdue them in Your wrath, O God!

9   You Yourself have counted my wanderings; put my tears in Your flask; record them in Your ledger.

10   Then my enemies will retreat on the day that I call out; this I know, that God is with me.

11   In God, in Whose attribute of judgment, I praise even what seems bad, in Hashem, in Whose attribute of mercy I praise the good.

12   In God, I have trusted, and therefore, shall not fear; what can man do to me?

13   I must fulfill my vow to You, O God; I will repay You with thanksgiving offerings.

14   For You have saved my soul from death and my feet from stumbling, to walk in God's presence in the light of the living.

PSALM FIFTY-SEVEN

Despite the tribulations, an expression of gratitude to Hashem

1. For the conductor, a plea to be spared from calamity, a sonnet by David that he wrote when he was fleeing from Saul in a cave:[15]

2. Be gracious with me, O God; be gracious with me, for I have taken refuge in You; I seek refuge in the shadow of Your wings until danger passes.

3. I will call to God, Supreme, to God Who fulfills all His promises to me.

4. He will send help from above and rescue me from the disgrace of the one who wants to devour me forever; God will send His compassion and His truth.

5. My soul is amidst lions whose tongues are burning with slander; their teeth are like spears and arrows, and their tongues are like a sharpened sword.

---

15 Psalms 57-59 all state, "… a plea to be spared from calamity," refer to King Saul's pursuit of David and the latter's subsequent hiding and escape; see I Samuel, Ch. 23-24

PSALM FIFTY-SEVEN

6   O God, from high in heaven, let Your glory be apparent over all the earth.

7   They have prepared a net to trap me and have warped my soul; they dug a pit to ensnare me, but they will forever fall into it themselves.

8   My heart is loyal to You, O God, to both Your attribute of stern judgment and Your attribute of mercy; therefore, I will sing and chant praise.

9   Awake, my soul! Awake, O harp and lyre! I will awaken the dawn.

10   I will thank You among the nations, O Lord; I will sing Your praise among the peoples.

11   For Your compassion is as vast as the heavens, and the truth of Your salvation reaches the uppermost realms.

12   O God, from high in heaven, let Your glory be apparent over all the earth.

PSALM FIFTY-EIGHT

A prayer for the downfall of enemies

1 For the conductor, a plea to be spared from calamity, a sonnet by David:

2 Are you silent when you should be speaking justice? Do you judge mankind equitably?

3 Even in your heart, you devise evil schemes against me; the earth shrinks under the weight of your crimes.

4 The wicked are estranged from the womb; the liars go astray even before they're born.

5 Their venom is like the venom of a snake; like a viper that deafens itself so it cannot hear…

6 Therefore, it won't hear the voice of the charmers, not even the most expert spellbinder.

7 God, smash the teeth in their mouth; shatter the fangs of the young lions, Hashem!

8 Let them evaporate like water and disappear; may His arrows strike them down.

9 May they be like a snail that leaves slime as it slithers away; like a stillborn child that will never see the sun.

10 Before the young briars turn into hardened thorns, He will sweep them away alive in a whirlwind.

11 The righteous person will rejoice upon seeing retribution befall his oppressors; he will wash his feet in the blood of the wicked individual.

12 Then people will say, "Truly, there is a reward for the righteous; there is Divine justice on earth."

PSALM FIFTY-NINE

A prayer for rescue, to thank Hashem afterwards

1. For the conductor, a plea to be spared from calamity, a sonnet by David, when Saul posted sentries to guard the house and kill him:[16]

2. Deliver me from my enemies, O God; strengthen me against those who rise up against me.

3. Rescue me from evildoers and save me from bloodthirsty men.

4. Look how they lie in ambush to trap me; fierce men gather against me; I have neither transgressed nor done them any wrong, as You know, Hashem.

5. I never harmed them, yet they rush to seize me; rouse Yourself on my behalf and see.

6. And You, Hashem, God, Master of Legions, God of Israel, arouse Yourself to make all the nations accountable; do not ever pardon any treacherous villains.

---

16 See I Samuel, 19:11

PSALM FIFTY-NINE

7   They return in the evening, howling like dogs that roam around the city.

8   They inform on me with their mouths; their lips are like swords, and they think that no one hears.

9   But You, Hashem, laugh at them; You mock all the nations.

10   Because of Saul's power, I await You, for only God can rescue me.

11   My compassionate God will come to my aid before my enemies overpower me; God will let me see the downfall of my oppressors.

12   Don't kill them, otherwise my people might forget; in Your might, send them into exile and remove them from their homes, wealth, and status, O Lord, our shield.

13   All this is because of their sinful mouths and the words on their lips; let them be trapped in their own arrogance because of the profanities and the lies that they spread.

14   Put an end to them in Your wrath; put an end to them and let them vanish; then let it be known to the ends of the earth that God rules over the House of Jacob.

PSALM FIFTY-NINE

15 They return in the evening, howling like dogs that roam around the city.

16 They wander around searching for food and complain if not satiated.

17 But I will sing about Your might and rejoice toward morning in Your compassion; for You have been a stronghold for me and a refuge on the day of my distress.

18 My Strength, to You I sing praise; for God is my stronghold, my compassionate God.

PSALM SIXTY

Hashem alone grants the power of victory and success

1. For the conductor, a sonnet by David based on the ruling of the Sanhedrin, instructing how to act against Aram:[17]

2. When he waged war with Aram Mesopotamia and Aram Tzobah, when Yoav made a preemptive strike against Edom in the Valley of Salt, killing twelve thousand.

3. O God, You have forsaken us, You have enabled enemies to breach our borders, You have been furious with us! Return to us!

4. You have made the Land of Israel tremble; You have shattered it; repair its fragments, for it is stumbling.

---

17 Aram claimed that as descendants of Laban, David and Yoav were breaching Jacob's pact with Laban (see Genesis 31:44-53), which stipulated that their descendants would not attack each other. David consulted with the Sanhedrin, who ruled that since Aram treacherously allied with Israel's enemies Moab and Edom, they were first to break the pact. As such, the Sanhedrin ruled that Israel could make a preemptive strike against Aram (see Midrash Tanchuma, Devorim, Ch. 3).

PSALM SIXTY

5   You have shown hardship to Your people and have given them wine to drink that clouds their hearts.

6   You have given trials and tribulations to those who revere You, to uphold Your truth forever.

7   In order to rescue Your beloved, let Your right hand rescue and answer me.

8   God spoke in His holiness that He would help me and I would rejoice; that I would parcel out Shechem and measure the Valley of Succoth for myself.

9   I will capture the lands of Gilead and Menashe; Efraim will be my stronghold to the north; the men of Judah will be my ministers.

10 Moab will be my wash basin; I'll cast my shoe on Edom; Philistia will be subservient to me.

11 Who will bring me to seize the fortified city? Who will lead me to Edom?

12 Is it not You, O God, Who until now has forsaken us, and have not gone forward with our forces?

13 From now on, help us against our adversaries, for human salvation is futile.

14 With God, we will prevail; He will crush our oppressors.

PSALM SIXTY-ONE

A prayer for attaining closeness with Hashem

1. For the conductor on the string ensemble, by David:

2. Hear my cry, O God, listen to my prayer.

3. I call to You from the ends of the earth, when my heart is overwhelmed with sorrow; lead me to a rock that is too high for me to climb on my own.

4. For You have been a refuge for me, a tower of strength in the face of the enemy.

5. May I dwell in Your tent in this world and the next; may I take refuge under Your protective wings forever.

6. For You, O God, have heard my vows; You have granted the inheritance to those who revere Your Name.

7. May You add longevity to the days of the king; may his years span generations.

8. May he dwell forever in God's Presence; may kindness and truth protect him.

9. Therefore, I will sing praise to Your Name forever as I fulfill my vows day by day.

PSALM SIXTY-TWO

Reward is according to each person's deeds

1. For the conductor, to be chanted by Yeduthun the Levite, a psalm by David:

2. My soul yearns silently for God alone; my salvation comes from Him.

3. He alone is my Rock and my salvation; He elevates me, so I will not suffer a severe setback.

4. How long will you plot treacherously against a man? All of you will be slain like a wall that's about to fall, like a fence that's knocked over.

5. But because of his lofty level, they scheme to topple him; they desire deceit; each of them forever blesses with their mouths, but inwardly, they curse.

6. My soul yearns silently for God alone, for my salvation comes from Him.

7. He alone is my Rock and my salvation; He elevates me, so I will not falter.

8. My salvation and dignity depend on God; I take shelter in God, the rock of my strength.

9   People, trust Him at all times; pour your hearts out to Him, for He is our refuge forever.

10   For people are naught; mankind is full of deceit; placed together on a scale, they weigh nothing.

11   Don't trust in thievery and don't place false hope in swindling; don't pay attention when they seem to bear fruit.

12   God spoke once, but I learned two things: strength belongs to God;

13   And second, lovingkindness is Yours, O Lord, to repay each person according to his deeds.

PSALM SIXTY-THREE

David's prayer while hiding from Saul and his army

1. A psalm by David as a fugitive in the Judean desert:[18]

2. O God, You are my God, I yearn for You! My soul thirsts for You, my flesh hungers for You, as if I'm in a parched and barren wilderness with no water.

3. Surely, as I basked in Your presence in the Sanctuary, seeing Your might and glory, my soul was satiated.

4. For Your lovingkindness is better than life; my lips will praise You.

5. Therefore, I will bless You as long as I live; in Your Name, I will uplift my hands in prayer.

6. As if my soul were delighting in rich delicacies, my mouth will praise You with joyous lips.

7. I remember You when I am going to bed and I think about You throughout the night.

---

18 See I Samuel, 23:14

PSALM SIXTY-THREE

8   For You have always been my help; I rejoice in the shelter of Your Presence.

9   My soul clings to You; Your right hand has held me up.

10 And those who ambush my soul in the darkness will enter the bowels of the earth.

11 May they be struck down by the sword; may they be food for the foxes.

12 And the king will rejoice in God; all who swear allegiance to Him will delight, for the mouths of the liars will be stifled.

PSALM SIXTY-FOUR

A prayer to be rescued from enemies

1 For the conductor, a psalm by David:[19]

2 O God, hear my voice calling out in prayer and save my life from enemy terror.

3 Hide me from the schemes of the wicked, from the assembly of evildoers.

4 For they sharpened their tongues like swords; they aim their poisoned words like arrows

5 to shoot in stealth at the innocent person; suddenly, they shoot at him, with no fear of anyone.

6 They encourage each other in their evil endeavor; when they converse, it's about laying traps in secret; they think that no one will see them.

7 They search for pretexts most thoroughly, and they harbor their evil designs in the depths of their hearts.

---

19 Rashi explains that David composed this psalm in his holy spirit of prophecy, foreseeing that his offspring would be thrown into a lion's den (see Daniel 6:17).

8   Then God will smite them like a sudden arrow that strikes them.

9   Their own tongue will be their downfall; all who see them shall shake their heads in derision.

10   And everyone shall fear, declaring that this is God's justice, and they will understand His doing.

11   The righteous one will rejoice in Hashem and take refuge in Him, and all the upright of heart will rejoice.

PSALM SIXTY-FIVE

Fortunate is the individual who recognizes Hashem's might in the world

1   For the conductor, a psalm by David, a song:

2   For You, God, Whose presence is in Zion, silence is praise; to You, all vows will be paid.

3   Since You hear prayer, all flesh will come to You.

4   When all types of wickedness overwhelm me, You pardon our transgressions.

5   Happy is the person whom You choose to bring close to dwell in Your courts; may he be satiated with the good of Your House, Your Holy Temple.

6   On behalf of Your righteousness, answer us with glorious deeds, God of our salvation; the source of trust for all inhabitants of the ends of the earth and the faraway seas.

7   In His power, He sets mountains in their place; He is girded in strength.

8   He calms the roaring seas, the roar of their waves, and the uproar of nations that seek to destroy us.

9 The inhabitants of the far corners of the earth are awed by Your wonders; You gladden people with the lights in the sky that appear morning and evening.

10 You are mindful of the earth and water it; You enrich it abundantly from God's streams overflowing with water; You prepare people's grain, You prepare for the whole world.

11 You saturate the furrows and soften the soil; the raindrops moisten the earth, and You bless the vegetation.

12 You crown the year of Your goodness, and Your clouds shower the world with abundance.

13 The clouds even shower the desert lands, and the hills gird themselves in joy.

14 The meadows are adorned with flocks of sheep, and the valleys are covered in cereal grass; they shout in glee and even sing.

PSALM SIXTY-SIX

Praising Hashem for His magnificent Divine Direction of all of creation

1   For the conductor, a song, a psalm; shout jubilantly to God, all the earth!

2   Sing the glory of His Name; make His praise glorious.

3   Say to God, "How glorious are Your deeds!" In fear of Your great strength, Your enemies will deny that they are Your enemies.

4   All the inhabitants of the earth will bow down to You, and they will sing praise to You; they will sing Your Name in praise forever.

5   Go and see the works of God; His acts inspire awe in people.

6   He turned the sea to dry land;[20] they crossed the river on foot;[21] there, we rejoiced in Him.

---

20   Splitting of the Red Sea; see Exodus, Ch.14
21   Splitting of the Jordan River; see Joshua, Ch.3

7   He rules mightily forever; His eyes monitor the nations; may the rebellious never applaud themselves.

8   O nations, bless our God! Make the sound of His praise be heard.

9   For He has kept us alive and prevented us from collapsing.

10   For You have tested us, O God; You have purified us as one purifies silver.

11   You have brought us into confinement; You have shackled our limbs with torment.

12   You placed foreign kings to rule over us; we've been through fire and water, but ultimately, You take us out to freedom.

13   I will come to Your Sanctuary with sacrificial offerings; I will fulfill my vows to You,

14   which my lips have uttered and my mouth has spoken when I was distressed.

15   I will offer fattened sacrificial offerings to You with the sweet smoke of rams; I will prepare sacrifices of young bulls and male goats always.

16   Come and listen, all those who revere God, and I will tell you what He did for my soul.

PSALM SIXTY-SIX

17 My mouth called out to Him, and His praise was on my tongue.

18 Had I harbored any evil in my heart, the Lord would not have listened.

19 Indeed, God did hear; He listened to the voice of my prayer.

20 Blessed is God, Who does not reject my prayer nor withhold His lovingkindness from me.

PSALM SIXTY-SEVEN

A prayer that the whole world should worship Hashem

1. For the conductor of the orchestra, a psalm, a song:

2. May God be gracious unto us and bless us; may He shine His face upon us forever.

3. So that Your way should be known on earth, Your salvation among all the nations.

4. Then the peoples will give thanks to You; the peoples will give thanks to You, all of them.

5. Nations will be happy and sing in joy, for You judge the peoples in equity and guide the nations on earth, forever.

6. Then the peoples will give thanks to You; the peoples will give thanks to You, all of them.

7. The earth will then yield its crop; may God, our God, bless us.

8. May God bless us and may all people to the ends of the earth revere Him.

PSALM SIXTY-EIGHT

A prayer for redemption and the downfall of our enemies

1 For the conductor of the orchestra, a psalm by David, a song:

2 God will arise, His enemies will scatter, and His foes will flee from His presence.

3 Just as smoke is dispersed, so will they be dispersed; like wax that melts in the presence of fire, so will the evil perish in the Presence of God.

4 But the righteous will rejoice; they will revel in the Presence of God and rejoice with delight.

5 Sing to God, chant praise to His Name; praise the One Who rides the heavens with His Name Ya'H[22] and be joyful in His presence.

6 Father of orphans and judge of widows is God in His holy domain.

---

22 This Holy Name, in Hebrew yud-hey, refers to the Name of Hashem that arouses the reverence of God (Rashi).

PSALM SIXTY-EIGHT

7   God brings singles into marriage; He releases those who were bound in chains, but the rebellious dwell in parched land.

8   O God, when You went out in front of Your people, when You marched them through the wilderness, forever;

9   the earth trembled and the heavens sweltered from the Presence of God; even Sinai shuddered from the Presence of God, the God of Israel.

10 You lavished a generous rain, O God; You sustain Your chosen people and promised land.

11 Your flock settled there; O God, in Your goodness, You provide for the needy.

12 The Lord made a declaration, a proclamation for all the nations.

13 Foreign kings and their armies will flee, and Israel, who dwells within the land, will divide the spoils.

14 Even if you now lie in humiliation, you will be like the wings of a dove that are coated in silver, its extremities in rare gold.

15 When the Almighty scatters the kings, the darkness will become bright.

PSALM SIXTY-EIGHT

16 The mountain of God is a choice mountain; the mountain of high peaks is a choice mountain.

17 Why do you prance, conceited high mountains? The mountain that God desires for His abode – there Hashem will reside forever.

18 God's chariot is twenty million angels; the Lord is among them, at Sinai in holiness.

19 You, Moses, ascended the firmaments; you captured the Torah from the angels and brought it as a gift to mankind so that Hashem may reside among the rebellious.

20 Blessed is the Lord, day by day; He bears our burden, the God of our salvation, forever.

21 God for us is a God of salvation, and the Lord Hashem[23] has many paths leading to the death of our enemies.

22 God will crush the head of His enemies, the hairy scalp[24] of he who walks around with his evil ways.

---

23 In the original Hebrew, this is the Ineffable Name, which indicates the attribute of mercy, but with the vowels of E'lohim, indicating stern judgment; in this manner, King David is showing that Hashem is merciful in judgment.

24 A reference to the empire of Edom, the descendants of the hairy Esau (see Genesis 25:25).

PSALM SIXTY-EIGHT

23   The Lord said, "I will retrieve Israel's dispersed from Bashan; I will bring them from the depths of the sea…

24   so that your foot will wade in the blood of your enemies; dogs' tongues will feed off of the enemies' corpses."

25   They saw Your ways, O God, at the Red Sea; the ways of my God, my King, in holiness.

26   First came the singers, then the musicians, in the midst of young girls playing timbrels.

27   The entire congregation blessed God; even unborn babies in the wombs of Israel sang to the Lord.

28   There is Benjamin, the youngest who rules them, followed by the princes of Judah who threw stones in jealousy[25] followed by the princes of Zebulun and the princes of Naftali.

29   Your God has endowed you with strength; be strong, O God, and dwell in the Sanctuary that You have already prepared for us.

---

25   The Tribe of Benjamin wanted to be the first to jump into the Red Sea; the Tribe of Judah was jealous and threw stones at Benjamin to delay them, so that Nachshon ben Aminadav, the president of Judah, could overtake them and be the first to jump into the Red Sea (Rashi, commentary on Psalm 114:2).

30 By virtue of Your sanctuary in Jerusalem, kings will bring gift offerings to You.

31 Rebuke Amalek, the nation that resembles a wild boar that lives among the reeds, the assembly of warriors who worship calves, the idols of nations who prostrate themselves to money; scatter the warmongering nations.

32 Then, when Moshiach comes, tribute-bearers will come from Egypt and Ethiopia and extend their hands to God.

33 Kingdoms of the earth, sing to God! Sing praise to the Lord, forever,

34 to Him Who rides upon the highest of the primordial heavens; indeed, He makes His supernatural voice a mighty voice.

35 Attribute might to God, Whose grandeur is upon Israel and Whose might is in the skies.

36 God, You are glorious from Your Sanctuaries! God of Israel, it is He Who bestows might and power to His people, blessed be God.

PSALM SIXTY-NINE

A prayer for salvation from the depth of tribulations

1. For the conductor, on behalf of a nation that resembles a rose among thorns, by David:

2. Save me, Hashem, for the floodwaters are up to my neck.

3. I am sinking in quicksand and cannot stand up; I am cast in deep waters, and the raging current is sweeping me away.

4. I'm exhausted from crying out; my throat is parched; my eyes are failing from looking so intensely to Hashem.

5. Those who hate me for no reason are more numerous than the hairs on my head; my enemies bearing false witness who want to eliminate me have become mighty; must I repay that which I never stole?

6. O God, You know my foolish deeds; my sins are not hidden from You.

PSALM SIXTY-NINE

7 Don't let me fall into the hands of my enemies so that others who await You, O Lord, God of Legions, won't be discouraged; let those who seek You, O God of Israel, not be humiliated because of me.

8 For Your sake, I have suffered disgrace; my face is enveloped in humiliation.

9 I seem weird to my brothers, like a foreigner to the sons of my mother.

10 They eat me alive because of my passion for Your Sanctuary; I have become the brunt of ridicule for those who scorn You.

11 And my soul wept while fasting, and they made fun of me for that too.

12 I dressed in sackcloth and became the brunt of their mockery.

13 The loiterers at the city gate gossip about me; the drunks in the beer halls sing in jest about me.

14 But as for me, may my prayer come to You, Hashem, at an auspicious moment; O God, in Your abundant lovingkindness, answer me with Your true salvation.

15 Rescue me from the mire so that I won't sink; save me from my enemies and from the deep waters.

16. Don't let the raging current sweep me away and don't let the depths of the sea swallow me and don't let the pit close its mouth over me.

17. Answer me, Hashem, for Your lovingkindness is good; turn to me in accordance with Your abundant mercy.

18. And don't hide Your face from Your servant for I am distressed; answer me quickly.

19. Come close to my soul and redeem it; rescue me so that my enemies will see Your power.

20. You are aware of my disgrace, my shame and my humiliation, for all my oppressors are revealed to You.

21. Disgrace has broken my heart, and I have become mortally sick; I longed for encouragement but there was none, and for someone to console me, but I didn't find anyone.

22. They even put gall in my food and gave me vinegar to drink.

23. May their own food be a death-trap for them and their dream of living in serenity backfire on them.

24. Let them lose their eyesight so they cannot see where they're going, so that their legs always stumble.

PSALM SIXTY-NINE

25 Pour out Your wrath on them, and may Your raging anger catch up with them.

26 May their home be desolate and their tents be forsaken.

27 The ones You struck slightly, they persecuted even more; they plotted how to make the ones whom You weakened suffer much more.

28 Let their sins collect and don't give them access to Your mercy.

29 May they be erased from the Book of Life, and may their names never be inscribed with the righteous.

30 But I am humbled and hurting, raise me up with Your salvation, O God.

31 I will praise the Name of God with song and exalt Him with thanksgiving.

32 And it will be gratifying to Hashem more than a ritual sacrifice of a full-grown bull with horns and hooves.

33 The humble will see and rejoice; seekers of Hashem – your hearts will be revived.

34 For Hashem hears the destitute and does not forsake His prisoners in exile.

PSALM SIXTY-NINE

35   Heaven and earth will praise Him, the seas and every living creature within them.

36   For God will redeem Zion and rebuild the cities of Judea and they shall settle there and inherit it.

37   The offspring of His servants will possess it and those who love His Name will abide within it.

PSALM SEVENTY

A prayer for immediate rescue from sufferings

1. For the conductor, by David, as a reminder to Hashem to hasten the salvation:

2. Rescue me, God! Hashem, come quickly to help me!

3. May those who seek to destroy my soul be shamed and disgraced; may those who seek to harm me retreat in humiliation.

4. Let them be appalled when disgrace comes back to them, those who ridiculed me and rejoiced in my troubles.

5. May all those who seek You be happy and rejoice in You; let those who love Your salvation always say, "May God be praised!"

6. As for me, I am poor and destitute; O God, come quickly! You are my help and deliverance; Hashem, do not delay!

PSALM SEVENTY-ONE

A prayer for rescue from enemies

1. I have trusted in You, Hashem; may I never be disappointed.

2. In Your benevolence, save me and rescue me; listen to my prayer and redeem me.

3. Be a sheltering rock that I can come to always; You gave the order to save me, for You are my Rock and my Fortress.

4. My God, save me from the hand of the evil and from the grasp of the unjust and the ruthless.

5. For You are my hope, O Lord God, in Whom I've trusted since my childhood.

6. From birth, I've relied on You; You took me out of my mother's womb; my praise is always about You.

7. I became an example to many, for despite all my troubles, You have been my shelter and strength.

8. My mouth will fill with Your praise, glorifying You all day long.

PSALM SEVENTY-ONE

9 Don't cast me away as I grow old; don't forsake me when my strength fails me.

10 For my enemies talk about me and those who monitor my every move conspire against me,

11 saying, "God has abandoned him; pursue him and seize him for there's no one to save him."

12 O God, don't be far from me; my God, hasten to help me.

13 Let those who despise me perish in shame; may those who seek my harm be enveloped in disgrace and humiliation.

14 As for me, I will always await Your salvation, and then I will add to all Your praise.

15 My mouth will tell of Your benevolent deeds, all day long of Your salvations, for I cannot begin to count them.

16 I will thank You, O Lord God, for Your mighty acts; I will celebrate Your righteousness, Yours alone.

17 O God, You have shown me Your miracles ever since I was a child, and to this day, I tell of Your wondrous deeds.

18 Even until old age and my final years, don't forsake me, O God, until I tell the next generation about Your strength, and to anyone who comes to me about Your might.

19 Your benevolence reaches the high heavens, O God; You have done magnificent things, O God – who is like You?

20 You, Who has shown me many severe troubles, revive me again and uplift me once more from the depths of the earth.

21 Enhance my status and turn to comfort me.

22 I will also thank You with the music of the harp for Your faithfulness, my God; I will sing praise to You with the lyre, Holy One of Israel.

23 My lips will rejoice as I sing praise to You, as well as my soul, which You have redeemed.

24 All day long, my tongue will tell of Your benevolent deeds, for those who seek my harm have been stifled and disgraced.

PSALM SEVENTY-TWO

Before King David departs the physical world, he prays for the success of his son Solomon[26]

1. A prayer for Solomon: O God, give the new king a heart that understands Your laws and enable this son of a king to judge in righteousness.

2. May he judge Your nation fairly and the poor with justice.

3. May the mountains bear peace for the nation and the hills yield abundance, in merit of people's charitable deeds.

4. May he be a champion of justice for the poor, save the children of the destitute, and crush the oppressor.

5. May they fear You as long as the sun and moon endure, for all subsequent generations.

6. May his words penetrate like rain on fresh-cut grass, like raindrops that drench the earth.

---

26   See I Kings, 2:1

7   May the righteous flourish in his generation, and may an abundance of peace endure as long as the moon.

8   May he rule from the Red Sea to the Mediterranean, from the Euphrates to the ends of the earth.

9   May governors bow down to him, and may his enemies bite the dust.

10 May the kings of Tarshish and the faraway islands repeatedly pay tribute; may the kings of Sheba and Saba offer gifts.

11 May all kings prostrate themselves before him; may all the nations serve him.

12 For he will save the destitute who cry out and the poor individual with no one to help.

13 He'll pity the needy and rescue the souls of the destitute.

14 He'll redeem their souls from fraud and violence; their blood will be precious to him.

15 May Hashem grant him life and vast wealth, pray for him always, and bless him all day long.

16 May there be an abundance of grain on earth, even on the mountaintops; may the plentiful fruit on the trees rustle in the wind like the cedars of Lebanon; may Jerusalem's population grow as numerous as blades of grass on earth.

17 May his name endure forever; may his name perpetuate as long as the sun; in his merit, all people will be blessed; they will praise him.

18 Blessed is Hashem, God, God of Israel, Who alone does wondrous deeds.

19 And blessed is His glorious Name forever, and may His glory fill the entire earth, amen and amen!

20 This is the closing prayer of David, the son of Jesse.

BOOK THREE

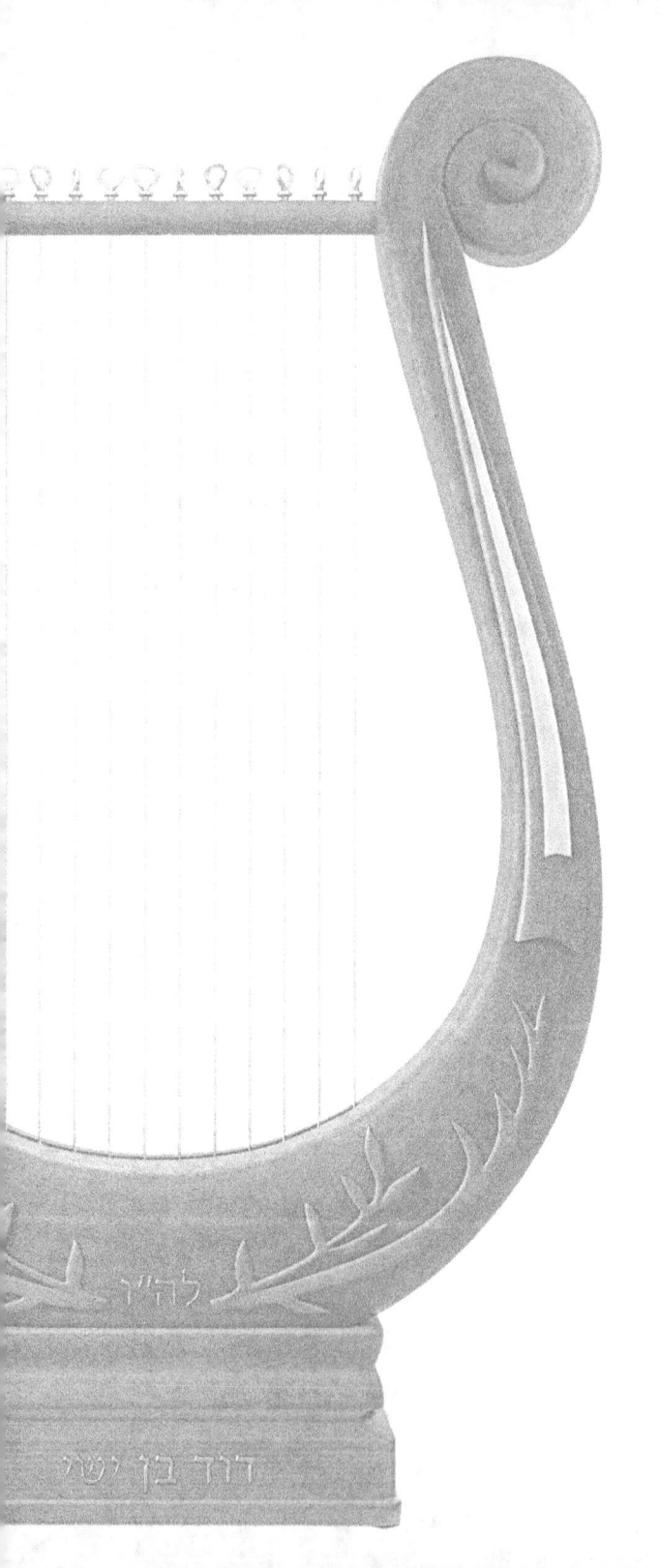

PSALM SEVENTY-THREE

Don't be jealous when the evil seems to succeed

1. A psalm by Asaph; surely God is good to Israel, to the pure of heart.

2. But before I understood this, I nearly slipped and strayed from the path.

3. For I envied the merrymakers when I saw the tranquility of the wicked.

4. For they have no premonition of death, and they enjoy prime health.

5. They don't toil like the masses and are not afflicted like the rest of mankind.

6. Therefore, they wear arrogance like a necklace, and they're clothed in violence.

7. Their eyes protrude from fat faces, and they fulfill their cravings even beyond their expectations.

8. They scoff and connive deceitful schemes; they talk as if they were on top of the world.

PSALM SEVENTY-THREE

9   Their mouths blaspheme Heaven and their tongue swaggers on earth.

10   They pull down the morality of the nation and regard the waters of Torah as wastewater.

11   And they say, "How can we believe that God knows anything? Is there awareness of what transpires down here in the Highest Realm?"

12   Look how the evil, who live in tranquility, amass huge wealth.

13   Have I purified my heart and cleaned my hands of sin in vain?

14   I am plagued with troubles all day long and chastised with tribulations every morning.

15   If I were to tell the reality of this generation, I would be betraying Your children.

16   So I strained to understand this Divine policy, but it seemed to be a hopeless task.

17   Until I came to God's Sanctuary and contemplated the fate of the wicked.

18   But the smooth path that You let them choose ends up in darkness and oblivion.

PSALM SEVENTY-THREE

19 How they've become desolate in a moment, swept away and terminated in terror.

20 Like a dream that disappears upon awakening, the Lord will arise and deface their image.

21 But my heart would cringe when I'd see the wicked succeed, and I struggled to understand,

22 for I was ignorant and unaware, like an animal that doesn't understand its master.

23 Still, I was always with You; You held my right hand.

24 May You guide me in Your counsel, and after I depart, take my soul to glory.

25 Whom else do I have in the heavens? And with You, I desire no one else on earth.

26 My flesh and my heart yearn for You; for You, O God, are my heart's strength and my portion for posterity.

27 See how those who distance themselves from You perish; You destroy all those who stray from You.

PSALM SEVENTY-THREE

28 As for me, being close to God is the ultimate good; I put my trust in the Lord Hashem,[27] to recount all of Your wondrous works.

---

27 In the original Hebrew, this is the Ineffable Name, which indicates the attribute of mercy, but with the vowels of E'lohim, indicating stern judgment; in this manner, King David is showing that Hashem's apparent stern judgment is nonetheless mercy.

PSALM SEVENTY-FOUR

A prayer for redemption from exile

1. By Asaph, retold in contemporary language by a wise orator: why, O God, have You abandoned us for what seems like an eternity? Why are You so angry at the sheep of Your flock?

2. Remember Your people whom You took for Your own, long ago; the tribe of Your heritage; the same Mount Zion, where You bestowed Your Presence.

3. Trample the enemy to eternal ruin for all the destruction of the Holy Temple.

4. Your oppressors made an uproar in the Temple and placed their symbols as signs of their success.

5. They wanted to swing their axes against the Heavenly Temple, but the wood swallowed their axes.

6. Even so, they hammer away at all the gates with iron tools of destruction.

7. They set Your Sanctuary on fire; they have desecrated the Tabernacle of Your Name to the ground.

PSALM SEVENTY-FOUR

8   All their leaders together resolved to burn all of God's meeting places on earth.

9   We saw none of the future signs promised to us, for there is not yet a prophet who can reveal the end, and no one knows how long the exile will last.

10 Until when, O God, will the oppressor blaspheme? Will the enemy denigrate Your Name forever?

11 Why do You restrain both of Your hands? Send Your right hand from Your midst and destroy the enemy.

12 For God is my King since the beginning of time, Who performs salvations down here on earth.

13 You shattered the sea with Your might; You smashed the heads of the Egyptians on the water.

14 You crushed the heads of Pharaoh and his officers, and gave their wealth to the nation that was heading to the wilderness.

15 You split open the wellspring and stream; You dried up the mighty rivers.

16 For the day is Yours and the night is Yours; You prepared the moon and the sun.

17 You established all the boundaries of earth; You prepared summer and winter.

18 Remember this: the enemy blasphemed Hashem and the indecent people desecrate Your Name.

19 Do not give the beasts the soul of Your dove; don't forget the lives of Your downtrodden forever.

20 Look at the covenant, for the dark places of our exile on earth have become havens of violence.

21 Don't shame the oppressed by rejecting their prayers; then, the poor and the destitute will praise Your Name.

22 Arise, O God, and fight Your battle! Remember how the indecent blaspheme Your Name all day long.

23 Don't forget the clamor of Your foes, the uproar of those who rise against You that ascends constantly.

PSALM SEVENTY-FIVE

A prayer for the future Redemption

1. For the conductor, a plea to be spared, a psalm by Asaph, a song:

2. We thank You, God, for the good; we thank You for the bad; Your name is in our mouths, and people have always told of Your wondrous works.

3. "At the time I choose for the Redemption, I will judge the enemies of Israel with exacting justice."

4. "The earth and all its inhabitants shall melt in fear; I have made its pillars firm forever."

5. I said to the scoffers, "Stop your mocking;" and to the evil, "Don't rule arrogantly."

6. Don't dare lift your haughty head skyward, blaspheming with an outstretched neck.

7. For greatness doesn't come from one's chasing money to the east or west, nor from one's dealings in faraway lands.

8. For God is the Judge; He lowers the haughty and uplifts the lowly.

9. For Hashem holds the cup of misfortune, like a cup of strong wine that has been mixed with bitterness; and He will pour the especially bitter sediment into cups that the evil on earth will drink.

10. For I will forever tell of His might; I will sing praise to the God of Jacob.

11. "For I will cut down the pride of the wicked." The esteem of the righteous will then be exalted.

PSALM SEVENTY-SIX

A prayer for the downfall of oppressors

1. For the conductor of the orchestra, a psalm by Asaph, a song:

2. God will be known in Judea; in Israel, His Name will be great.

3. For His Sanctuary will be in Jerusalem and His dwelling place in Zion.

4. There, He will break the fiery projectiles, the shield, the sword, and all instruments of war, forever.

5. You eradicate enemies; You are mightier than the predators who are as gigantic as mountains.

6. The stout-hearted warriors will be dumbfounded, like in a deep sleep; none of the troops will be able to lift a finger.[28]

---

28 According to Rashi, this is a reference to Hashem's miraculous salvation when the Assyrians laid siege against Jerusalem in the time of King Hezekiah, and Hashem destroyed them in their sleep (see Kings II, 19:37).

PSALM SEVENTY-SIX

7   At Your admonition, O God of Jacob, the horse and the chariot were immobilized.

8   You are so very glorious! Who can remain standing in the face of Your fury?

9   From the heavens, Your judgments will resonate; the earth will tremble with fear, then become silent,

10   when God arises to pass judgment and to save the earth's humble people forever.

11   For the rage of the wicked will cause mankind to thank You; You will neutralize any remnant of their power.

12   Make vows and fulfill them to Hashem, your God; let all the neighboring countries bring tribute to the Revered One.

13   He will shrink the spirit of the arrogant; the leaders of the world will fear Him.

PSALM SEVENTY-SEVEN

A prayer for the end of exile

1. For the conductor, to be chanted by Yeduthun the Levite, Asaph's psalm.

2. I lift my voice to God and cry out; I lift my voice to God and He listens to me.

3. On the day of my distress, I seek the Lord; my wound does not heal the whole long night of exile; my tears flow incessantly, and my soul refuses to be comforted.

4. I recall the acts of kindness that God would do for me, and I sigh; when I speak, shall my soul be enveloped in sorrow forever?

5. You held my eyelids open all night long; I was so upset that I could not speak.

6. I pondered the days of old, the years long past.

7. During the night, I would remember the melody from the Holy Temple; I'd speak to my heart, and my soul would search for understanding.

8. Will You abandon us forever, O Lord? Can we no longer appease You?

9   Has Your lovingkindness terminated for posterity? Is this a decree that You will be angry forever?

10   Has God forgotten forgiveness? Has anger sealed off His mercy forever?

11   And I tell myself that the change of the Divine aspect of mercy to stern judgment is to arouse fear.

12   I recall the works of God, for I remember Your wonders of old.

13   I contemplate everything You do and will speak about Your wondrous deeds.

14   O God, Your way is to sanctify Your Name; what god is as great as God?

15   You are the God who works wonders; You have revealed Your might among the nations.

16   With Your powerful arm, You redeemed Your people, the sons of Jacob and Joseph, forever.

17   The waters saw You, O God; the waters saw You and were terrified; even the depths trembled.

18   Clouds poured water, the skies thundered, and even arrows of lightning flew all around.

PSALM SEVENTY-SEVEN

19   Thunder rumbled in the whirlwind, lightning bolts lit up the world; the earth quaked and roared.

20   You paved a way in the sea, a lane in the mighty waters, but You left no imprint behind.

21   You led Your nation like a flock in the hand of Moses and Aaron.

PSALM SEVENTY-EIGHT

A call to remember Hashem's wondrous acts

1. By Asaph, retold in contemporary language by a wise orator: listen, my people, to my teaching; pay close attention to what my mouth is saying.

2. I open my mouth with a parable; I will allude to the lessons of the past.

3. The things that we have heard and are aware of their authenticity, for our fathers told us.

4. We also will not withhold them from our children, recounting the praises of Hashem until the final generation, all about His might and the wondrous things He did.

5. And Hashem presented the testimony to His greatness before the Congregation of Jacob and gave the Torah to Israel, which He commanded our fathers to observe His laws and to pass them down to future generations,

6. so that the final generation may know; children yet to be born will arise to tell their own children;

7. so that they'll put their trust in God and never forget the wondrous acts to safeguard His commandments.

PSALM SEVENTY-EIGHT

8   To prevent them from being a rebellious and disobedient generation like their fathers, a generation whose heart was misaligned and whose spirit lacked faith in God.

9   The sons of Ephraim, although armed and skilled archers, fled in retreat on the day of battle.

10   They did not observe God's covenant and refused to follow His Torah.

11   And they forgot His acts and His wondrous deeds that He showed them.

12   In the presence of their fathers, He performed amazing things in the land of Egypt, in the field of Tzo'an.

13   He split the sea and took them through it and made the waters stand upright like a wall.

14   He led them by a cloud during the day and by the light of a fire at night.

15   He cracked open boulders in the desert and provided abundant water as if it came from the deep wellsprings.

16   He gathered streams from a boulder and made them flow like river rapids.

17 But they still continued to sin, to defy the Most High in the parched wilderness.

18 And they tested God in their hearts, demanding food to fulfill their craving.

19 And they spoke against God, saying, "Can God set a table in the wilderness?"

20 "Sure, He struck a rock and water flowed and streams gushed out; but can He provide bread also? Can He prepare meat for His people?"

21 Then Hashem heard and was extremely angry; a fire erupted against Jacob and fury flared up at Israel.

22 Because they didn't believe in God, nor did they trust in His salvation.

23 So He commanded the skies above and opened the doors of heaven.

24 And He rained down manna for them to eat, giving them the bread of heaven.

25 Humans ate the bread of angels; He sent them their provisions until everyone was satiated.

26 He unleashed the east wind from the heavens and powerfully steered the south wind.

PSALM SEVENTY-EIGHT

27   He rained meat on them like dust; flying fowl like the sand of the sea.

28   The quail landed in the middle of the camp, all around their tents.

29   They ate and were excessively satiated, for He gave them what they craved.

30   They had yet to stop craving with the food still in their mouths,

31   when God's anger flared up at them and He slew their biggest gluttons and felled the young men of Israel.

32   Nevertheless, they continued to sin and refused to believe in His wondrous deeds.

33   He ended their days in futility and their years in sudden death.

34   When He killed them, the others would seek Him, repent and pray to God.

35   And they would remember that God is their Rock and the Supreme God is their Redeemer.

36   But they would entice Him with their mouths, but lie to Him with their tongues.

37 And their hearts were insincere with Him, and they were unfaithful to His covenant.

38 Even so, He in His mercy forgave wickedness and didn't destroy them, and repeatedly curbed His anger, not arousing His entire wrath.

39 For He remembered that they were mere flesh and blood, here today and gone tomorrow.

40 How many times they defied Him in the desert and grieved Him in the wilderness!

41 And they repeatedly tested God, challenging the Holy One of Israel.

42 They did not remember His mighty hand, the day He redeemed them from the Egyptian oppressors.

43 The phenomenal signs that He placed on Egypt, and His wonders in the field of Tzo'an.

44 He turned their rivers into blood and rendered their waters undrinkable.

45 He sent swarms of wild beasts to devour them and frogs to destroy them.

46 And He gave their crops to the grasshoppers and the yield of their labors to the locust.

PSALM SEVENTY-EIGHT

47   He destroyed their vines with hail and their sycamores with cicadas.

48   He handed their cattle over to the hailstones and their flocks to the fire within the hail.

49   He sent the products of His fierce disgust upon them; the plagues of fury, wrath and calamity; an entourage of evil angels.

50   He paved a path for His anger and did not spare their souls from death, and handed over their lives to a plague.

51   And He smote every firstborn in Egypt; the first fruits of their vigor in the tents of Ham.

52   And He prodded His people like sheep, guiding them like a flock in the wilderness.

53   And He led them securely so they wouldn't fear, and the sea overwhelmed their enemies.

54   Then He brought them to His sacred border, to the mountain that His right hand had formed.

55   Then He drove away the Canaanite nations before them and apportioned them their land inheritance and settled the tribes of Israel in their tents.

56 Yet they tested and defied the Supreme God and did not observe His commandments.

57 And they fell away and became unfaithful like their fathers, shifting to serve false gods like a bow that shoots in the wrong direction.

58 They angered Him with their elevated altars and provoked Him with their idols.

59 God heard and was enraged; He was extremely disgusted with Israel.

60 He abandoned the Tabernacle of Shilo, the tent where He resided among men.

61 He allowed the holy Ark of the Covenant to fall into the hands of the Philistines and His splendor into the hands of oppressors.

62 He handed His people over to the sword and harbored extreme displeasure against His inheritance.

63 Fire devoured His young men, and therefore His maidens had no wedding.

64 His priests fell by the sword, and His widows could not weep.

65 Then the Lord awoke as if He were asleep, like a warrior rousing from wine.

PSALM SEVENTY-EIGHT

66   And He beat His enemies into retreat, giving them eternal disgrace.

67   And He was repulsed with the tent of Joseph and no longer chose the Tribe of Ephraim.

68   And He chose the Tribe of Judah and Mount Zion that He loves.

69   And He built His Temple like the high heavens and like the earth, established it forever.

70   And He chose His servant David and took him from the sheep corrals.

71   He brought him from behind the nursing ewes to tend to Jacob, His nation, and to Israel, His chosen.

72   And he tended to them in accordance with the purity of his heart and led them by the skill of his hands.

PSALM SEVENTY-NINE

An appeal to Hashem to give our enemies what they deserve

1. A psalm by Asaph; heathens have entered Your domain, have desecrated Your holy Sanctuary, and have turned Jerusalem into mounds of ruins.

2. They have given the corpse of Your servants as food for the birds in the sky and the flesh of Your pious ones to the wild animals on earth.

3. They shed their blood like water all around Jerusalem, and there was no one to bury them.

4. We became a disgrace to our neighbors, the object of scorn and derision for all the nations that surround us.

5. Until when, Hashem, will You be forever angry, with Your indignation burning like a fire?

6. Pour Your wrath on the nations that have not recognized You and on the kingdoms that have not called Your Name.

7. For they have devoured Jacob and desolated his sanctuary.

PSALM SEVENTY-NINE

8   Don't hold our prior sins against us; quickly, extend Your mercies to us, for we are extremely destitute.

9   Help us, O God of our salvation, for the sake of Your glorious Name, rescue us and atone for our sins for the sake of Your Name.

10 Why should the nations say, "Where is their God?" May the nations know, and we see with our own eyes, the revenge of Your servants' spilled blood.

11 May the prisoner's cry of agony come before You; as befits Your strong arm, release those who are condemned to death.

12 Repay our neighbors sevenfold in their midst, the disgrace that they disgraced You, O Lord.

13 As for us, we are Your people, the sheep of Your flock; we will thank You forever and tell of Your praise from generation to generation.

PSALM EIGHTY

A prayer for the future Redemption

1. For the conductor, testimony about the future of the nation that resembles roses among thorns, Asaph's psalm:

2. Listen, O Shepherd of Israel, You who leads Joseph like a flock; You, Whose Presence abides among the angels, appear to us!

3. Arouse Your might before Ephraim, Benjamin and Menashe, for it is befitting for You to save us.

4. O God, bring us back from exile and shine Your face on us to redeem us.

5. Hashem God, Master of Legions, until when will You fume at the prayers of Your people?

6. You fed them the bread of tears and gave them a huge cup of tears to drink.

7. You put us in conflict with our neighbors and our enemies mock us.

8. O God, Master of Legions, bring us back from exile and shine Your face on us to redeem us.

PSALM EIGHTY

9   You brought a grapevine out of Egypt, expelled nations, and planted it.

10   You cleared the land for it, its roots took hold, and it filled the land.

11   Its shadow covered the mountains, and its branches became mighty cedars.

12   Its branches stretched to the sea and its tender shoots as far as the Euphrates.

13   Why have You breached its fences so that every passerby can pluck its fruit?

14   The wild boar from the forest gnaws away at it, and an insect in the field feeds on it.

15   O God, Master of Hosts, please return; look down from heaven and see – attend to this vine,

16   and the cutting that You planted with Your right hand and on the one that You have taken as Your own.

17   It is now scorched in the fire and felled, perishing from Your angry rebuke.

18   Grant a helping hand to Your right-hand man, the one that You have taken as Your own.

PSALM EIGHTY

19 Don't push us away from You; revive us and we will call Your Name.

20 O God, Master of Legions, bring us back from exile and shine Your face on us to redeem us.

PSALM EIGHTY-ONE

A song of praise for miracles of Rosh Hashanah

1. For the conductor, on the lyre that comes from Gat, by Asaph:

2. Sing joyously to God, our strength; shout out to the God of Jacob.

3. Raise your voice in song and sound the drum, the melodious lyre with the harp.

4. Blow the shofar on the occasion of the new moon, at the appointed time of our festival day.

5. As it is law for Israel, a directive from the God of Jacob.

6. He made it a testimony for Joseph, for on that day he went out to rule over the land of Egypt, "A language I did not know, I suddenly understood."

7. I removed the burden from his shoulders and freed his hands from the cauldron of slavery.

8. You called out in distress and I rescued you; you called privately, but I answered you with a thunderous voice; even though I know you will sin again, I nonetheless save you forever.

9 Hear, My people, and I will bear witness to you; Israel, if only you would listen to Me.

10 There will not be a strange god within you, and you will not bow down before an alien god.

11 I Am Hashem Your God who brings you up from the land of Egypt; open your mouth wide with a request and I will fulfill it.

12 But My people did not heed My voice, and Israel did not want to hear Me.

13 So I sent them away in their stubbornness and let them follow their own wicked counsels.

14 If only My people would heed my voice, and Israel would walk in My ways.

15 Then I would instantly subdue their enemies and turn My hand on their oppressors.

16 Those who hate Hashem deny Him, but their doom will be eternal.

17 And He will feed His people Israel the finest wheat and satiate them with honey from a rock.

PSALM EIGHTY-TWO

A reproof of judges who warp justice

1. A psalm by Asaph; God's Presence is in the midst of the judges to see whether they judge truthfully.

2. Until when will you judge unjustly? And, will you show favor to the rich and powerful forever?

3. Dispense justice for the needy and the orphan; vindicate the poor and the impoverished.

4. Rescue the needy and the destitute and save them from the hand of the wicked.

5. The judges neither know nor understand that they walk in darkness; they cause the foundations of the earth to collapse.

6. I said that you are like Divine beings, all of you the sons of the Most High.

7. Nevertheless, you will die as mortals and you will fall like one of the corrupt ministers.

8. Arise, O God, and judge the earth for all of the nations are Your possession.

PSALM EIGHTY-THREE

A prayer for rescue from our enemies

1   A song, A psalm by Asaph:

2   O God, don't be silent; don't be deaf to the taunts of our enemies and don't be still, O God.

3   See how Your enemies are making an uproar and those who hate You have lifted their heads.

4   They secretly conspire against Your people and scheme against those who take refuge in You.

5   They said, "Let us go and annihilate them as a nation so that the name Israel will no longer be remembered."

6   They are unanimous in their conspiracy, for they have made an alliance against You.

7   The tents of Edom, Ishmael, Moab and the sons of Hagar.

8   Gebal, Ammon and Amalek; Philistia with the inhabitants of Tyre.

PSALM EIGHTY-THREE

9   Even Assyria has joined them; they became the eternal allies of the sons of Lot.

10 Deal with them as You did to Midian, like Sisera and Jabin at the Kishon river.[29]

11 They were destroyed at Ein Doar, trampled like fertilizer for the earth.

12 Put their nobles like Orev and Zeev, and like Zevah and Zalmuna and all their princes,[30]

13 who said, "We will conquer God's haven for ourselves."

14 O my God, make them like dandelion fluff, like chaff in the wind;

15 like a fire burning the forest and like a flame that sets the mountains ablaze.

16 In like manner, pursue them with Your storm and terrify them with Your hurricane.

17 Fill their faces with shame until they seek Your Name, Hashem.

---

29 See Judges, Ch. 4
30 Midianite leaders whom Gideon destroyed, see Judges, Ch. 7-8

18 Let them be humiliated and horrified, disgraced and doomed forever.

19 And they will know that You – Your Name is Hashem – are alone Supreme over all the earth.

PSALM EIGHTY-FOUR

A prayer for redemption

1. For the conductor, on the lyre that comes from Gat, by the sons of Korach, a psalm.

2. How cherished is Your Holy Sanctuary, Hashem, Master of Legions.

3. My soul yearns, even craves for the courtyards of Hashem; my heart and my flesh sing out in prayer to the living God.

4. Even the bird finds a home and the sparrow a nest to lay her baby birds, near Your Sanctuary, Hashem, Master of Legions, my King and my God.

5. Happy are those who dwell in Your house; indeed, they will praise You forever.

6. Happy is the person who puts his trust in You, whose heart contemplates the ways to serve You.

7. But the transgressors who pass through the grave, making it like a river with all their tears, now understand that those who chastised them wanted to bestow blessings on them.

PSALM EIGHTY-FOUR

8   But those who progress from strength to strength in Divine service will appear before God in Zion.

9   Hashem, God, Master of Legions, hear my prayer; listen, O God of Jacob, forever.

10   Remember our shield, the Holy Temple, O God, and look at the face of David, Your anointed, who toiled to build it.

11   For one day in Your courtyards is better than a thousand years elsewhere; I prefer to stand at the entrance of Your house rather than dwell in luxury in the tents of wickedness.

12   For Hashem our God is our illumination and shield; Hashem bestows grace and glory; He will not withhold goodness from those who walk in the path of innocence.

13   Hashem, Master of Legions, happy is the person who trusts in You.

PSALM EIGHTY-FIVE

A prayer for redemption

1. For the conductor; composed by the sons of Korach, a psalm:

2. Hashem, You cherish Your land, especially when You return Your exiled nation of Jacob.

3. You have forgiven the wickedness of Your people; You have buried all their sin forever.

4. You have retracted Your entire wrath; You have rescinded Your fury.

5. Return us, God of our salvation, and revoke Your anger at us.

6. Will You be agitated with us forever? Will Your anger persist from generation to generation?

7. Surely, You will revive us again and Your people will rejoice in You.

8. Hashem, show us Your lovingkindness and grant us Your salvation.

PSALM EIGHTY-FIVE

9   May I merit to hear what Hashem the Almighty will speak; for He will speak peace to His nation and to His pious ones, and they will not return to their folly.

10   His salvation is certainly close to those who revere Him, so that His glory may abide in our land.

11   Lovingkindness and truth have met, righteousness and peace have embraced.

12   Truth will emerge from the land, and justice will reflect from the heavens.

13   Hashem will also provide the good, and our land will yield its harvest.

14   Let every person walk in righteousness, and may it become the path of his footsteps.

PSALM EIGHTY-SIX

A prayer to be rescued from distress

1. A prayer by David: Hashem, incline Your ear; answer me, for I am poor and destitute.

2. Guard my soul, for I am devout; save Your servant, for You are my God and I trust in You.

3. Favor me, O Lord, for I call out to You all day long.

4. Gladden the soul of Your servant, for I lift my soul to You, O Lord.

5. For You, O Lord, are good and forgiving and exceedingly kind to those who call out to You.

6. Lend an ear to my prayer, Hashem, and listen to the voice of my prayers.

7. I will call out to You on the day of my distress, for You will answer me.

8. No power is comparable to You, O Lord, and there is nothing like Your deeds.

9 All the nations that You have made will come and bow down before You, O Lord, and will give honor to Your Name.

10 For You are great and work wonders; You alone are God.

11 Teach me Your ways, Hashem; I will walk in the path of Your truth; unify my heart to revere Your Name.

12 I will thank You with all my heart, O Lord my God, and I will honor Your Name forever.

13 For Your compassion to me is great and You have saved my soul from the depths of the grave.

14 O God, malicious men have risen up against me and a band of brutal people has sought my soul, and they are not mindful of You.

15 But You, O Lord, are the merciful and forgiving God, slow to anger and abundant in lovingkindness and truth.

16 Turn to me and be gracious to me; give Your strength to Your servant and save the son of Your maidservant.

17 Show me a sign of Your favor so that my enemies will see and be humiliated, for You, Hashem, have helped me and consoled me.

PSALM EIGHTY-SEVEN

The praise of Jerusalem

1. A psalm by the sons of Korach, a song that is based on Mount Zion and Jerusalem;

2. Hashem loves the gates of Zion more than all the dwellings of Jacob.

3. Glorious things are spoken about you, O city of God, forever.

4. I remind my acquaintances of Egypt and Babylon; here is Philistia and Tyre with Ethiopia, boasting about a great person who was born there.

5. But in the future, every person born in Zion will be praised. For Hashem will establish it as supreme among the cities.

6. Hashem, in the future when He writes the verdicts of all the nations, He will count those of Israel who were exiled among them and say, "These were born in Zion," and separate them forever.

7. Then the singers and dancers will chant, "All my soul rejoices in Your salvation."

PSALM EIGHTY-EIGHT

A prayer for the People of Israel in exile

1. A song, a psalm by the sons of Korach for the conductor on the responsive tambourine, retold in contemporary language by a wise orator, Heman the Ezrachi:

2. Hashem, God of my salvation, I cry out to You day and night.

3. May my prayer come before You; lend Your ear to my prayer.

4. For my soul is bursting with troubles, and my life has reached the grave.

5. I am considered like those who have already descended to the grave; I have become a man with no strength,

6. among the dead who are free, like corpses lying in the grave whom You no longer revive, for they were cut down by Your hand.

7. You put me in the deepest pit, in the dark places of the depths.

PSALM EIGHTY-EIGHT

8 Your anger weighed down heavy on me and all Your waves of tribulations have tormented me.

9 You have isolated me from my acquaintances; You have made me detestable to them; I am imprisoned and cannot leave.

10 My eyes are sore from affliction; I called out to You every day, Hashem, and have outstretched my hands to You.

11 Will You work wonders for the dead? Will the deceased arise to thank You forever?

12 Shall Your lovingkindness be told about from the grave, and Your faithfulness from the place of oblivion?

13 Shall Your wonders become known from the darkness, or Your righteousness from a forsaken wasteland?

14 As for me, I have cried out to You, Hashem, and my prayers greet You every morning.

15 Why do You neglect my soul, Hashem, hiding Your face from me?

16 From youth, I am afflicted and dying; I bear Your fearful judgment wherever I turn.

PSALM EIGHTY-EIGHT

17   Your anger has overwhelmed me; Your shocking terror has uprooted me.

18   They surround me like water, all day long; together, they besiege me.

19   You have distanced both friend and companion from me, as if my acquaintances were concealed in darkness.

PSALM EIGHTY-NINE

A prayer for the return of David's kingdom

1. A psalm retold in contemporary language by a wise orator, Eitan the Ezrachi:

2. I will sing of Hashem's lovingkindness forever; my mouth will inform every generation of Your faithfulness.

3. For I thought that a world of compassion would be built and the Heavens would fulfill Your promise.

4. "I made a covenant with My chosen one; I swore to David, My servant."

5. "I will perpetuate your seed forever and I will build your throne from generation to generation, forever."

6. And the heavens will acknowledge Your wonders, Hashem, and Your faithfulness in the congregation of the holy people.

7. For who in the sky can equal Hashem? And who among the mighty powers can compare to Him?

8. God is praised in the great counsel of the holy angels and held in utter awe by all those who surround Him.

PSALM EIGHTY-NINE

9 Hashem, O God, Master of Legions, who is like You, mighty God? Your faithfulness surrounds You.

10 You rule over the sea's grand waves; when they rise, You knock them down.

11 You broke Egypt into a lifeless force; with the might of Your arm, You scattered Your enemies.

12 The heavens are Yours and the earth is Yours too; You established the world and everything in it.

13 North and south, You created them; Tabor and Hermon rejoice in Your Name.

14 Yours is the arm with power; Your hand is strong, Your right hand is praised.

15 Righteousness and justice are the foundation of Your throne; lovingkindness and truth accompany You.

16 Happy is the nation that knows the sound of the shofar; Hashem, they will walk in the light of Your face.

17 They will rejoice in Your name all day long and are uplifted by Your righteousness.

18 For You are the magnificence of their power; through Your will, our prestige will be elevated.

PSALM EIGHTY-NINE

19 For our shield belongs to Hashem and our king to the Holy One of Israel.

20 Then You spoke in a vision to Your devout prophets, and said: "I have bestowed my assistance on the hero, I have exalted the chosen one from among the people."

21 I found My servant David and have anointed him with My holy oil.[31]

22 My hand will assist him and My arm will strengthen him.

23 The enemy will not overcome him nor will the villain torment him.

24 I crush those who oppress him and afflict those who hate him.

25 And My faithfulness and lovingkindness are with him and in My Name shall his esteem be uplifted.

26 And I will place his dominion over the sea and his right hand over the populace of faraway rivers.

---

31 Verses 21-38 is Hashem speaking.

27 He will call Me, "Father, You are my God and the Rock of my salvation."

28 I will make him like a first-born, supreme over all the kings of the earth.

29 I forever reserve My lovingkindness for him and My covenant will remain faithful to him.

30 And I have placed his offspring on his throne forever, and I have made his throne like the days of the heavens.

31 If his offspring will forsake My Torah and fail to walk in the path of My laws;

32 if they profane My statutes and fail to observe My commandments;

33 then I will punish their transgression with the rod, and their wickedness with afflictions;

34 but I will not rescind My compassion from him nor will I falsify My promise to him.

35 I will not violate My covenant nor will I go back on My word.

36 I have sworn one oath by My holiness, that I will not disappoint David.

PSALM EIGHTY-NINE

37 His offspring will endure forever and his throne will be as lasting as the sun before Me.

38 Like the moon, his throne shall endure forever as the celestial bodies are faithful witnesses for posterity.

39 But You have forsaken and rejected them, the offspring of Your anointed.

40 You nullified the covenant of Your servant and have cast his crown to the ground.

41 You have breached all his fences and turned his fortresses into debris.

42 All the wayfarers have trampled him, and he became a disgrace to his neighbors.

43 Your right hand has uplifted his oppressors, and You have gladdened all his enemies.

44 You even dulled the edge of his sword and failed to uphold him in battle.

45 You terminated his grandeur and cast his throne to the ground.

46 You shortened the days of his youth; You enveloped him in shame for what seems to be an eternity.

PSALM EIGHTY-NINE

47 Until when, Hashem, will You hide from us forever with Your wrath burning like a fire?

48 I remember how brief my life is; have You created all of humanity for no reason?

49 Who is the individual who will live and not see death, whose soul can escape the grave forever?

50 Where are Your original acts of lovingkindness, O Lord, the ones that You pledged to David in Your faithfulness?

51 Remember, O Lord, the disparagement of Your servant that I carry in my midst and suffer from an entire multitude of nations;

52 that Your enemies have disgraced us and disgraced the footsteps of Your Moshiach.

53 Blessed is Hashem forever, amen and amen.

BOOK FOUR

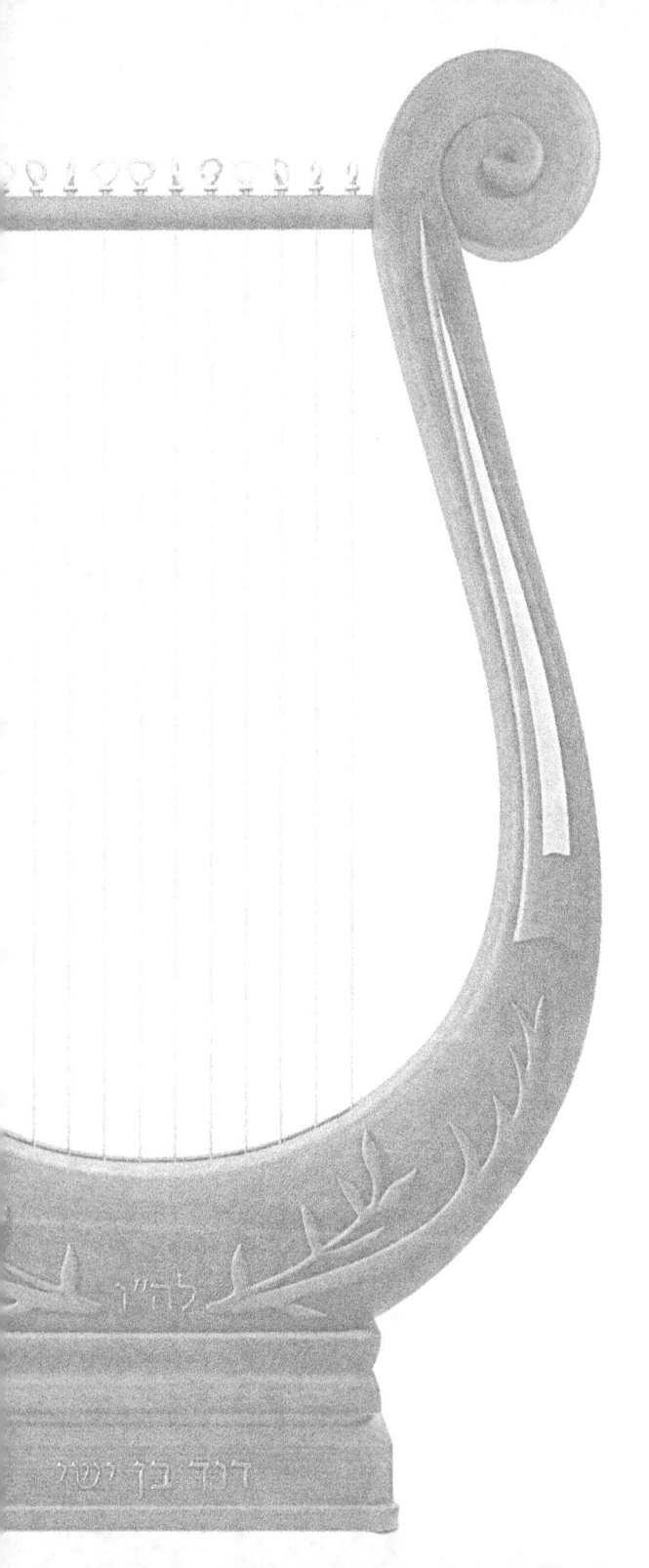

PSALM NINETY

*A prayer for Redemption and the return
of the Divine Presence*

1   A prayer by Moses,[32] the man of God; Lord, You have been our shelter in every generation.

2   Before the mountains were formed and before You created the earth and the inhabited land, You are God from the infinite past to the infinite future.

3   You bring a person to sorrow and say, "Repent, you children of mankind."

4   For a thousand years are to You like a fleeting yesterday, not even like a few hours of night.

5   Their lives flow past them like a night's sleep; in the morning, they're like withered grass.

---

32   Moses originally said Psalms 90-100. The Gemara (tractate Bava Basra, 14b) cites that King David incorporated the works of ten elders in the Book of Psalms: 1) Adam; 2) Malki-tzedek; 3) Abraham; 4) Moses; 5) Heman; 6) Yeduthun; 7) Asaph; 8-10) Three sons of Korach.

PSALM NINETY

6   In the morning, it sprouts and rejuvenates, but by evening, it is dry and brittle.

7   For we are devoured in Your anger and shocked by Your wrath.

8   You have placed our sins in front of You; the sins of our youth in the light of Your face.

9   All of our days have transpired in Your anger; because of our sins, we wasted our years like a sigh.

10 Our longevity is seventy years, and with added strength eighty years, and even great success is none other than pain and toil, for it terminates quickly, and we fly away.

11 Who can fathom the power of Your anger? As You are feared, so is Your anger.

12 Teach us to use our days productively so we can acquire a heart of wisdom.

13 Come back, Hashem! Until when will You be angry at us? Think favorably of Your servants.

14 Satiate us in the morning with Your lovingkindness, and then we shall sing out and rejoice throughout all of our days.

PSALM NINETY

15 Gladden us in accordance with the days that You afflicted us, the years when we saw suffering.

16 May Your deeds be apparent to Your servants and Your glory to their children.

17 May the pleasantness of the Lord our God be upon us and the work of our hands be enduring; may the work of our hands endure.

PSALM NINETY-ONE

The virtues of trust in Hashem

1. Whoever takes refuge in the Most High dwells under the Almighty's protective shadow.

2. I will say to Hashem, "You are my shelter and my stronghold; in my God, I shall trust."

3. For He will rescue you from the trapper's net, from the devastating plague.

4. He will cover you and you will find shelter under His wings; His truth is a shield and armor.

5. You shall not fear the terror of night nor the arrow that flies during the day;

6. nor the plague that lurks in the dark nor the menace that destroys at noon.

7. Even though a thousand demons are positioned at your left and ten thousand on your right, they will not approach you.

8. You will merely look with your own eyes, and you'll see the retribution of the wicked.

PSALM NINETY-ONE

9 Because you said, "Hashem, You are my shelter," you have made the Most High the abode of your trust.

10 No evil will befall you, nor will any pestilence come near your tent.

11 He commands His angels on your behalf, to guard over you wherever you go.

12 They will carry you in their palms so that your foot won't hit a stone.

13 You will tread on the lion and on the viper; you will trample the young lion and the snake.

14 For he has yearned for Me and I will rescue him; I will elevate him because he knows My Name.[33]

15 He will call Me and I will answer him; I Am with him in times of trouble; I will not only rescue him but bring him honor as well.

16 I will satiate him with length of days, and I shall show him My salvation.

---

33 Hashem is speaking in verses 14-16.

PSALM NINETY-TWO[34]

Gratitude for and praise of Hashem's Divine Direction of the world

1. A psalm, a song for the Sabbath day:

2. It is good to thank Hashem and to sing praise to Your Name, high above everything.

3. To tell of Your lovingkindness by day and of Your faithfulness by night.

4. On a ten-string harp and on the lyre, on a harp with a vocal accompaniment.

5. For You have gladdened me with Your doings, Hashem; I rejoice at the works of Your hands.

6. How great are Your works, Hashem! Your thoughts are exceedingly profound.

7. An ignorant person will not know, nor can a fool understand this.

---

34 Adam said this psalm on the first Sabbath of creation; this is therefore the first song of praise ever sung to the Almighty. Moses renewed this psalm in his generation.

8   When the evil sprout like blades of grass and all the purveyors of wickedness blossom, it's to destroy them forever.

9   And You are glorious forever, Hashem.

10 For here are Your enemies, Hashem; behold, Your enemies will perish; the purveyors of wickedness will be dispersed.

11 You uplift my esteem like the horns of antelopes; You anoint me with invigorating oil.

12 My eyes will see the downfall of the enemies that monitor me; when those who would harm me rise up against me, my ears will hear of their setback.

13 A righteous person flourishes like a date palm and grows tall like a cedar of Lebanon.

14 Planted in the House of Hashem, in the courtyards of our God, they will flourish.

15 They will still be fruitful in old age, remaining vigorous and fresh,

16 to declare that Hashem is just, my Rock in Whom there is no injustice.

PSALM NINETY-THREE

Once Moshiach comes, the whole world will recognize Hashem's Monarchy

1. Hashem is King, He is dressed in grandeur; He is dressed and has fortified Himself in power; the world is firmly established and will no longer be shaken.

2. Your throne was established from before the beginning of time; You are eternal.

3. The enemies of Hashem raise their voices like raging rivers; the rivers uplift their roaring.

4. But more than the roar of many waters, mightier than the big breakers of the ocean, You are mighty above everything.

5. The testimonies of Your prophets about Your House, the Sacred Dwelling, are very trustworthy; Hashem, may it be everlasting.

PSALM NINETY-FOUR

A prayer for redemption

1. Hashem, God of vengeance; God of vengeance, appear!

2. Arise, Judge of the earth; give the arrogant what they deserve.

3. Hashem, until when will the evil, until when will the evil gloat?

4. They open their mouths in arrogance; all these evildoers prance around in pride.

5. They oppress Your people, Hashem, and terrorize Your chosen.

6. They kill the widow and the convert, and they murder orphans.

7. And they say that the Lord doesn't see and the God of Jacob doesn't understand what they're doing.

8. Understand, you senseless among the nations; fools, when will you acquire wisdom?

PSALM NINETY-FOUR

9   He Who implants the ear, will He not hear? He Who creates the eye, will He not see?

10 He Who chastises nations, will He not reprimand? It is He Who teaches men knowledge.

11 Hashem knows the vanity of man's thoughts.

12 Happy is the man whom Hashem chastises, yet You teach him Your Torah,

13 to give him respite from the days of evil until a pit is dug for the wicked.

14 For Hashem will not forsake His people nor abandon His chosen.

15 For justice comes back to the righteous, and afterwards, all the upright of heart will receive their reward.

16 Who will get up to defend me against evildoers? Who will stand up for me against the purveyors of wickedness?

17 Were it not for Hashem's help, my soul would have dwelt silent in the grave already.

18 If I said that I'm about to collapse, Your lovingkindness, Hashem, held me up.

19 When negative thoughts almost overwhelmed me, Your consolations gladdened my soul.

20 Can a throne of a falsehood connect with You, those who turn injustice into law?

21 They band together to kill a righteous person and condemn the blood of the innocent.

22 But Hashem became a stronghold for me, and my God, the Rock of my shelter.

23 And He turned their own evil designs against them and will destroy them with their own wickedness; Hashem, our God, will destroy them.

PSALM NINETY-FIVE

A call to praise Hashem

1. Come, let us sing to Hashem, let us shout in joy to the Rock of our salvation.

2. Let's greet Him with thanksgiving, joyfully shout to Him in songs of praise.

3. For Hashem is a great God and a great King above all heavenly powers.

4. For in His hand is all of creation, from the depths of the earth to the summits of the mountains.

5. The sea is His, for He created it, and His hands fashioned the dry land.

6. Come, let us bow down and kneel, let us bend the knee before Hashem, our Maker.

7. For He is our God and we are His people, the flock He tends to, today, if only we would listen to Him.

PSALM NINETY-FIVE

8 Don't harden your hearts like you did in Merivah,[35] the day you tested Hashem in the desert.

9 When your forefathers tried Me; they tested me even though they had seen My works.

10 For forty years, I was perturbed with that generation; and I said that they are an errant-hearted people, for they have not known My ways.

11 Therefore, I swore in My anger that they shall not enter the Land of My Sanctuary.

---

35 See Exodus 7:1-7

PSALM NINETY-SIX

The future joy in the world when all nations recognize Hashem's sovereignty

1. Sing a new song to Hashem; sing to Hashem, everyone on earth.

2. Sing to Hashem, bless His Name; tell each other about His salvation every day.

3. Tell of His glory among the nations and of His wonders among all peoples.

4. For Hashem is magnificent and exceedingly praised; He is held in awe by all the heavenly powers.

5. For all the gods of the nations are mere idols, but Hashem made the heavens.

6. Glory and majesty are in His Presence, strength and splendor in His Sanctuary.

7. Give tribute to Hashem, O families of nations; attribute to Hashem power and glory.

8. Give tribute to Hashem the honor that is worthy of His Name; bring an offering and come to the courtyards of His Temple.

9   Bow down to Hashem in His exceedingly Holy Temple; tremble in His Presence, all the earth.

10   Declare among the nations, "Hashem has reigned." The world stands firm, it will not collapse; He will judge the nations with equity.

11   Let the heavens rejoice and the earth exult; may the sea and everything in it thunder with praise.

12   The fields and everything in them will exult; then, all the trees of the forest will sing in joy,

13   in the Presence of Hashem, for He is coming; He is coming to judge the earth; He will judge the world with justice and the peoples with His truth and faithfulness.

PSALM NINETY-SEVEN

Amalek and his offspring will no longer prevail

1. Hashem has reigned, let the world rejoice; let the inhabitants of the faraway islands be glad.

2. Dense clouds surround Him; righteousness and justice are the foundation of His throne.

3. Fire is His strike force and blazes all around His enemies.

4. Lightning bolts illuminate the globe; the earth saw and trembled.

5. Mountains melted like wax in Hashem's Presence; in the presence of the Lord of all the earth.

6. The heavens declare His righteousness, and all the nations see His glory.

7. All the idol worshippers who take pride in their worthless deities will be humiliated; bow down to Him, all the heavenly beings.

8. Zion heard and rejoiced; the cities of Judea exulted because of Your judgments, Hashem.

9 For You, Hashem, are supreme over all the earth; extremely exalted above all the heavenly beings.

10 Those who love Hashem, despise evil; He guards the lives of His pious ones and saves them from the hand of the wicked.

11 Light is destined for the righteous and joy for the upright of heart.

12 All you righteous, rejoice in Hashem, and give thanks to His holy Name.

PSALM NINETY-EIGHT

The song celebrating the future Redemption

1. A psalm; sing a new song to Hashem for He has performed wonders; His right hand and His holy arm have brought redemption.

2. Hashem showed His salvation to the whole world, for He has revealed His righteousness in full sight of the nations.

3. He remembered His lovingkindness and faithfulness to the House of Israel; all the far corners of the earth have seen the salvation of our God.

4. Shout out to Hashem, all the earth; sing joyous songs and play music.

5. Sing praise to Hashem with the lyre; with the lyre and with the voice of melodious song.

6. With the trumpet and the sound of the shofar, call out in the presence of Hashem the King.

7. The sea and everything in it will roar; the earth and all its inhabitants will rejoice.

8 The rivers will clap their hands; the mountains together will rejoice,

9 in the presence of Hashem, for He is coming to judge the earth; He will judge the world with justice and the peoples with equity.

PSALM NINETY-NINE

The downfall of Gog and Magog

1. Hashem has reigned, the nations will tremble; the earth will quake before Him, Who is enthroned upon the angels.

2. Hashem is great in Zion and exalted above all the peoples.

3. They will acknowledge Your great and glorious Name, for it is holy.

4. Mighty is the King, for He loves justice; He established equity; You made Jacob's attributes of justice and righteousness.

5. Praise Hashem our God and bow at His Sanctuary, for He is holy.

6. Moses and Aaron among His priests and Samuel, who called His Name, they called to Hashem and He answered them.

7. He spoke to them from the pillar of a cloud, for they observed His commandments and the law that He gave them.

PSALM NINETY-NINE

8   Hashem, our God, You answered them; for them, You have been a forgiving God in their merit, but You exact retribution for their misdeeds.

9   Exalt Hashem our God and bow at His holy mountain, for Hashem our God is holy.

PSALM ONE HUNDRED

A call to give thanks to Hashem

1. A psalm of thanksgiving; call out to Hashem, all the earth.

2. Serve Hashem with gladness, come before Him with joyous song.

3. Know that Hashem is God; He made us and we are His, the flock of His pasture.

4. Enter His gates with thanksgiving, His court with praise; thank Him and bless His Name.

5. For Hashem is good, His compassion is everlasting, and His faithfulness endures from generation to generation.

PSALM ONE HUNDRED ONE

David's wonderful character and demeanor

1. A psalm of David; whether in times of compassion or in times of stern judgment, I will sing; to You, Hashem, I sing praise.

2. I will seek to understand the way of wholeheartedness; when will You come to me? I will act with a pure heart even in the privacy of my home.

3. I refuse to look at anything evil; I despise crooked dealings and want no part of them.

4. May my heart be devoid of perversion; I will not know evil.

5. I will obliterate those who defame their neighbor behind his back; I can't stand a person with haughty eyes and an arrogant heart.

6. I seek the trustworthy of the land to dwell with me; he who walks the way of integrity shall serve me.

7. He who deals in deceit will not dwell in my house; one who tells lies will not last in my presence.

PSALM ONE HUNDRED ONE

8 Every morning, I'll remove all the wicked of the land, to purge the City of Hashem from all evildoers.

PSALM ONE HUNDRED TWO

A prayer during times of trouble

1. A poor man's prayer, on the verge of collapse, when he pours out his heart to Hashem:

2. Hashem, hear my prayer and let my cry of anguish reach You!

3. Don't hide Your face from me on the day of my distress; listen to my prayer on the day that I call You, answer me right away.

4. For my days have gone up in smoke, and my bones are as dry as if burned in a furnace.

5. My heart is as withered as dry grass, for I am emaciated from not eating.

6. From the sound of my moaning, my skin clings to my bones.

7. I am like an owl of the desert, like a barn owl among the ruins.

8. I look at myself, and I've become like a lonely bird on a roof.

PSALM ONE HUNDRED TWO

9   My enemies disparage me all day long; those who deride me curse my name.

10   For my bread tastes like ash; my drink is diluted with my tears.

11   Because of Your fury and Your wrath, You uplifted me but then You threw me down.

12   My days are like a lengthening shadow and I wither away like grass.

13   But You, Hashem, are enthroned forever and Your Name is known from generation to generation.

14   And You will arise to show mercy on Zion, for it is time to pardon her, for the appointed hour has come.

15   For Your servants have always cherished her stones and have enamored her dust.

16   Then the nations will fear the name of Hashem, and all the kings of the earth will revere Your glory.

17   For Hashem will have built Zion, and His glory will be apparent there.

18   He was attentive to the prayer of the despondent and did not spurn their prayer.

19 Let this be recorded for the final generation so that the reborn nation will praise Hashem.

20 For He observed from His holy heights; Hashem looked from heaven to the earth;

21 to hear the prisoner crying in agony, to liberate those condemned to death;

22 so they can proclaim His Name in Zion and His praise in Jerusalem;

23 when all the nations gather together and kingdoms unite to serve Hashem.

24 He diminished my strength on the way and has shortened my days.

25 I say, "My God, don't take me away in the middle of my life, You Whose years endure throughout all generations."

26 In the beginning, You laid the earth's foundation, and the heavens are the works of Your hands.

27 They will perish but You will endure; they will all wear out like an old garment; You will change them like clothing and they all pass away.

PSALM ONE HUNDRED TWO

28   But You are God; Your years never end.

29   The sons of Your servants shall settle in their land and their offspring will endure in Your Presence.

PSALM ONE HUNDRED THREE

A wonderful prayer for the sick, thanking Hashem for all of His goodness

1. By David: bless Hashem, O my soul; all my internal organs, bless His Holy Name!

2. Bless Hashem, O my soul, and don't forget all of His favors.

3. He forgives all of your sins; He heals all of your ailments.

4. He redeems your life from the pit; He envelops you in lovingkindness and mercy.

5. He satiates your mouth with goodness so that you will be rejuvenated like an eagle.

6. Hashem performs charitable deeds and judgments to aid all of the downtrodden.

7. He made His ways known to Moses[36] and His actions to the Children of Israel.

---

36 These are the 13 Attributes of Divine Mercy (see Exodus 34: 6-7); several of them are mentioned in the coming passages of this Psalm.

PSALM ONE HUNDRED THREE

8   Hashem is merciful and forgiving, slow to anger and
    full of compassion.

9   He will not quarrel forever nor hold a grudge
    for posterity.

10 He doesn't treat us in accordance with our sins nor
    repay us in accordance with our sins.

11 For as high as the sky is above the earth, so great is
    His lovingkindness for those who revere Him.

12 As distant as east is from west, so has He distanced
    our transgressions from us.

13 As a father is merciful to his children, Hashem has
    been merciful to those who revere Him.

14 For He knows our natural inclinations and remembers
    that we are mere dust.

15 A human's days are like quickly-drying grass; as fast as
    he sprouts, he quickly flowers and then dries out.

16 For his spirit passes through him and is suddenly
    gone, and he no longer recognizes where it once was.

17 And Hashem's lovingkindness is forever and ever
    upon those who revere Him and His generosity for
    the children of their children,

18 for those who guard His covenant and for those who remember His commands to observe them.

19 Hashem has established His throne in Heaven, and His kingdom reigns over all.

20 Bless Hashem, His angels, the powerful warriors that do His bidding and heed the voice of His word.

21 Bless Hashem, all His legions, His servants who do His will.

22 Bless Hashem, all His works in all the places of His dominion; bless Hashem, O my soul!

PSALM ONE HUNDRED FOUR

Thanks to Hashem for all of His creations

1. Bless Hashem, O my soul; Hashem, my God, You are exceedingly great! You are dressed in glory and majesty.

2. You wear a robe of light and spread the heavens like a curtain.

3. His upper chambers have a roof of water; the clouds are His chariot, and He walks upon the wings of the wind.

4. He makes the winds His messengers and the flaming fire His servants.

5. He established the earth on its foundations so that it will stand firmly forever and ever.

6. You covered the earth with deep waters like a garment; the waters even covered the mountains.

7. The waters fled from Your rebuke; they hurriedly departed from the sound of Your thunder.

8. They ascended mountains, they descended valleys, to the particular place that You designated for them.

9 You placed a boundary that they may not overstep, so that they won't return to cover the earth.

10 He sends the wellsprings into the streams that flow between the mountains.

11 They water all the animals of the field and quench the thirst of the wild creatures.

12 The birds of the sky dwell near them and sing from the branches of the trees.

13 He waters the mountains from the clouds above; the land is satiated from the fruit of Your works, the rainclouds.

14 He sprouts the grasses for animal fodder and the grains through human labor to bring bread from the earth,

15 and wine that gladdens a person's heart, oil to make one's face glow, and bread that sustains the human heart.

16 The trees of Hashem drink their fill, the cedars of Lebanon that He planted.

17 There, the birds make their nests; the stork makes the cypress trees its home.

PSALM ONE HUNDRED FOUR

18 The high mountains are for the ibex, and the boulders are a refuge for the rock rabbits.

19 He made the moon for the festivals; the sun knows its destination.

20 You put the darkness in place and it is night, when all the creatures of the forest stir.

21 The young lions roar for their prey, asking the Lord for their food.

22 The sun rises and they return to rest in their dens.

23 Man goes out to his work, to toil until the evening.

24 How abundant are Your works, Hashem; with wisdom, You made them all; the earth is full of Your possessions.

25 This is the ocean, so great and expansive, with innumerable creatures, living things great and small.

26 There, the ships sail; the domain of the Leviathan, which You created to play with.

27 All of them look to You in hope, to provide them with their food in its proper time.

28 You give it to them and they gather it; You open Your hand and they are satiated with good.

29 If You hide Your face, they panic; if You retrieve their spirits, they die and return to their dust.

30 When You send forth Your breath, they are created and the face of the earth is renewed.

31 May Hashem's glory endure forever; may Hashem rejoice in His works.

32 He gazes at the earth and it trembles; He touches the mountains and they emit smoke.

33 I will sing to Hashem while I live; I will praise God as long as I endure.

34 May my words gratify Him; I will rejoice in Hashem.

35 May there be no more sins on earth and no more evil people; bless Hashem, O my soul, Halleluyah!

PSALM ONE HUNDRED FIVE

Praising Hashem for all His gifts, especially the gift of the Land of Israel

1. Give thanks to Hashem, call His Name; tell all the nations about His deeds.

2. Sing to Him, make music to Him, speak of all His wonders.

3. Glorify His holy Name; may the heart of those who seek Him be happy.

4. Turn to Hashem and His might; seek His presence always.

5. Remember the wonders that He has performed, His marvels and what He commanded us with His own mouth.

6. O offspring of Abraham, His servant; O children of Jacob, His chosen ones.

7. He is Hashem, our God; His judgments extend across the entire earth.

8 He remembers His covenant forever, a commitment He made to a thousand generations,[37]

9 that He made with Abraham[38] and His oath to Isaac;[39]

10 that He established as law with Jacob and a covenant for posterity with Israel;

11 saying, "I will give the Land of Canaan to you as your allotted inheritance."

12 When they were only a few in number, recent arrivals there.

13 And they wandered from nation to nation, from one kingdom to another.

14 He allowed no one to rob them and rebuked kings on their behalf.

15 "Don't touch My anointed ones; do no harm to My prophets."

16 And He declared a famine on earth and destroyed every source of bread.

---

37 Deuteronomy 7:9
38 Genesis 15:18
39 Ibid, 26:4

PSALM ONE HUNDRED FIVE

17   He sent a man ahead of them; Joseph was sold as a slave.[40]

18   They shackled his feet in chains and tormented his soul behind iron bars.

19   Until the time when his word came true and Hashem's decree purified him.

20   The king ordered to release him, a ruler of peoples to set him free.[41]

21   He made him master of his household and ruler of all his assets.

22   To make his ministers subordinate to Joseph, who taught wisdom to Pharaoh's elders.

23   And so Israel came to Egypt and Jacob resided in the Land of Ham.

24   And He made His nation exceedingly fruitful, growing mightier than its oppressors.[42]

---

40   Ibid, 37:27
41   Ibid, Ch. 41
42   Exodus 1:7

25 He turned the Egyptians' hearts around to hate His people and to plot against His servants.

26 He sent His servant Moses, with Aaron, whom He had chosen.

27 They implemented His signs among them and wonders in the land of Ham.

28 He sent darkness, and it became dark, and the plagues did not defy His word.[43]

29 He turned their waters into blood and killed their fish.

30 The land swarmed with frogs, even in the chambers of their kings.

31 He spoke, and hordes of wild animals came, with lice throughout their borders.

32 He turned their rain into hailstones of flaming fires in their land.

33 It struck their vines and their fig trees, and it felled the trees within their borders.

---

43   Ibid, Ch. 10

PSALM ONE HUNDRED FIVE

34 He spoke and the locust came, and innumerable grasshoppers.

35 And it devoured every blade of grass in their country and consumed the fruit of their land.

36 And He smote every firstborn in their land, the first fruit of their vigor.

37 And He took them out with silver and gold, and there was not even a single poor person in His tribes.[44]

38 Egypt rejoiced when they left for the dread of Israel had fallen upon them.

39 He spread out a cloud for shelter and a fire to illuminate the night.[45]

40 Israel asked and He brought them quail, satiating them with heaven-sent bread.[46]

41 He opened a rock and waters gushed out, flowing like a river through the dry wilderness.[47]

---

44 Exodus, Ch. 12
45 Ibid, Ch. 13
46 Ibid, Ch. 16
47 Ibid, Ch. 17

42 For He remembered the holy word that He gave to Abraham, His servant.[48]

43 And He took His people out with glee, His chosen with joyous song.

44 And He gave them the lands of nations,[49] and they inherited the possessions of peoples,

45 for the purpose of safeguarding His laws and observing His teachings, Halleluyah!

---

48 Genesis 15: 13-14
49 Exodus 3:17

PSALM ONE HUNDRED SIX

Hashem's magnificent compassion on our forefathers, despite their sins

1. Halleluyah! Give thanks to Hashem, for He is good, for His lovingkindness is eternal.

2. Who is capable of describing Hashem's mighty acts? Who can express all of His praise?

3. Fortunate are those who uphold Torah justice and perform charitable deeds at all times.

4. Remember me, Hashem, when You look at Your people favorably; include me in Your salvation.

5. May I merit seeing the good of Your chosen ones, to rejoice in the joy of Your nation, and to be praised together with the people You took for Your own.

6. We have sinned like our fathers; we have committed wickedness and acted wickedly.

7   Our forefathers in Egypt ignored Your wonders; they disregarded Your many acts of lovingkindness and rebelled by the sea at the Red Sea.[50]

8   And Hashem saved them for the sake of His Name, to reveal His might.

9   And He castigated the Red Sea, and it dried up. And He led them through the depths as if it were a desert.[51]

10 And He saved them from the hand of the enemy and redeemed them from the hand of the adversary.

11 And the waters covered their oppressors; not a single one of them was left.

12 And they believed in Him and sang His praise.[52]

13 They quickly forgot His deeds and did not turn to Him for advice.

14 And they were seized with craving in the desert and tested God in the wilderness.

---

50 Ibid, 14:11
51 Verses 9-11 recount Exodus 14:15-31
52 Refers to *Shirat Hayam*, the Song of the Sea, see Exodus 15:1-21

PSALM ONE HUNDRED SIX

15   Hashem granted their request and gave them quail but emaciated their soul.

16   And they were envious of Moses in the camp, and of Aaron, Hashem's holy one.[53]

17   The earth opened and swallowed Dathan and submerged the assembly of Abiram.

18   And a fire burned in the midst of their assembly; a flame consumed the wicked.

19   They made a golden calf in Horeb and bowed down to an idol.[54]

20   They exchanged God's Glory for the likeness of a grass-eating bull.

21   They forgot God, their Redeemer, Who did great things in Egypt,

22   wonders in the Land of Ham, glorious things by the Red Sea.

---

53   Verses 16-18 refer to Korach's rebellion, see Numbers, Ch. 16
54   Verses 19-23 refer to the golden calf fiasco, see Exodus, Ch. 32-33

PSALM ONE HUNDRED SIX

23 Hashem considered destroying them, had not His chosen one Moses intervened in their behalf to mitigate Hashem's wrath.

24 They scorned the promised land and had no faith in Hashem's word.[55]

25 And they whined in their tents and did not heed Hashem's voice.

26 And He raised His hand in an oath against them to smite them in the desert;

27 to exile their offspring among the nations and disperse them among the lands.[56]

28 They joined in the idolatry of Baal Peor and ate the sacrifices of the spiritually dead.[57]

29 And they angered Hashem with their misdeeds, and a plague broke out within them.

---

55 Verses 24-27 refer to the sin of the spies, see Numbers, Ch. 13-14
56 On the night of Tisha B'Av, Israel whined and complained when swayed by the spies. This day became a day of calamity throughout the generations, when both Temples were destroyed, and Israel was exiled among the nations.
57 Verses 28-31 refer to Numbers, Ch. 25

PSALM ONE HUNDRED SIX

30 And Phinehas intervened in prayer and in judgment, and the plague came to a halt.[58]

31 And the merit of this righteous deed is to his credit for every generation, forever.

32 They angered Hashem at the Waters of Strife, and Moses suffered because of them.[59]

33 For they went against Hashem's will[60] as He expressed with His lips.[61]

34 They did not destroy the nations as Hashem had commanded them.

35 Instead, they mingled with the nations and learned their ways,

36 and worshipped their idols, which became a stumbling block for them.

---

58 Numbers 25:7-8

59 Verses 32-33 refer to Numbers 20:1-13

60 Hashem commanded Moses and Aaron to talk to the rock, so that water would flow forth. This would have been a great sanctification of Hashem's Name. But in a moment of impatience, they hit the rock instead.

61 Hashem vowed that Moses and Aaron would not be entitled to enter the Land of Israel.

37 And they sacrificed their sons and daughters to the demons.

38 They spilled innocent blood, the blood of their sons and daughters that they sacrificed to the Canaanite idols; and the land was desecrated with spilled blood.

39 They became defiled by their deeds and went astray by their actions.

40 Hashem's wrath was kindled against His people, and He loathed His inheritance.

41 So He delivered them to the hands of nations, and their enemies ruled over them.

42 Their adversaries oppressed them, and they succumbed to their power.

43 Hashem saved them so many times but they relapsed to their evil ways; their wickedness brought them down.

44 But Hashem saw their distress when He heard their outcry.

45 And He remembered His covenant with them and relented as befits His abundant compassion.

46 Hashem caused all their captors to have mercy on them.

PSALM ONE HUNDRED SIX

47 Redeem us, Hashem our God, and gather us from among the nations to give thanks to Your Holy Name and to glorify ourselves by praising You.

48 Blessed is Hashem the God of Israel from this world to the world to come, and let all the people say, amen, Halleluyah!

BOOK FIVE

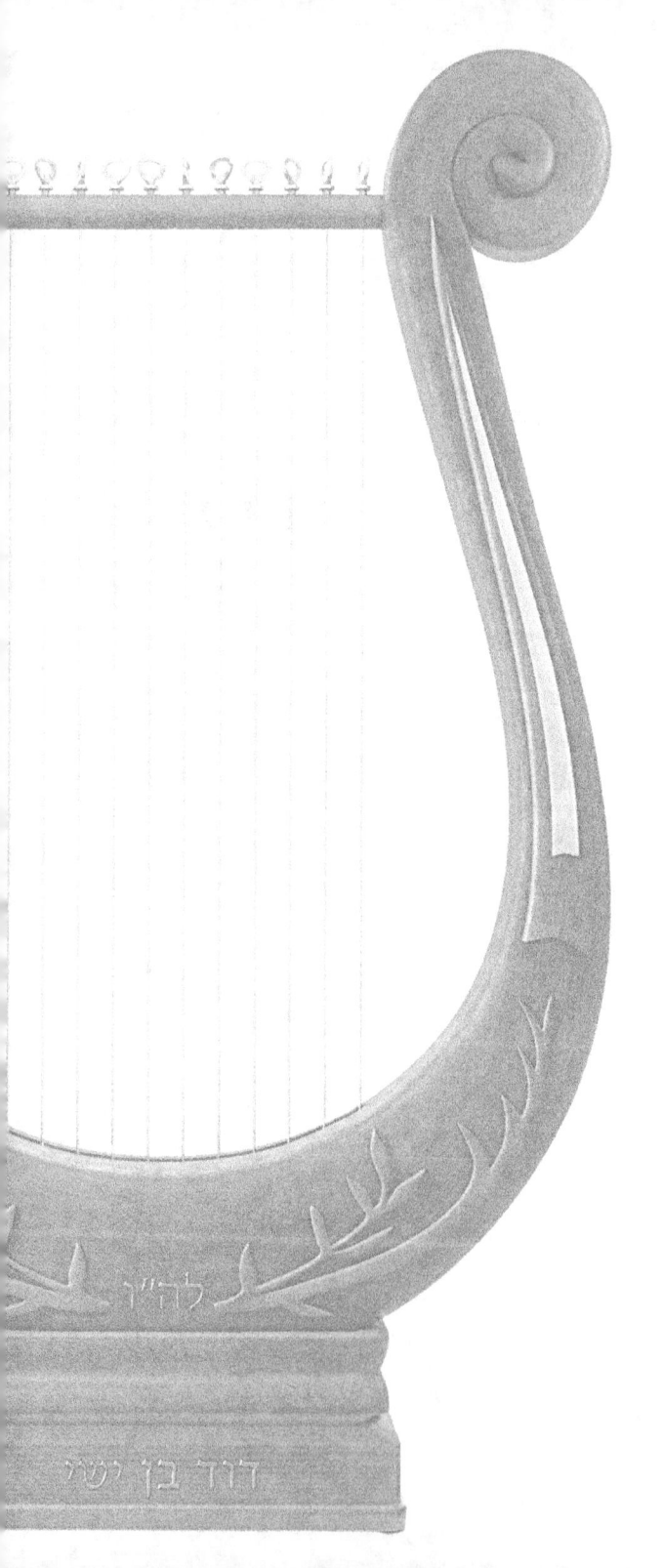

PSALM ONE HUNDRED SEVEN

Anyone who is rescued from danger must give thanks to Hashem

1 Give thanks to Hashem, for He is good;[62] His lovingkindness endures forever.

2 Let those whom Hashem saved say that they were rescued from the hand of distress;

3 and those whom He gathered from the lands – from east, west, north, and the south sea islands.

4 They lost their way in the barren wilderness and found no inhabited city.

5 They were hungry and thirsty, and their soul became faint within them.

6 Then they cried out to Hashem in agony, and He rescued them from their perils.

---

62 Psalm 107, the psalm of thanksgiving, mentions four cycles of peril and deliverance, which constitute the four groups who are required to thank Hashem for rescuing them. They are: 1) the desert traveler (verses 3-6); 2) the prisoner (verses 10-16); 3) the sick person (verses 17-22); and 4) the seafarer (verses 27-32).

PSALM ONE HUNDRED SEVEN

7   And He led them on a straight path that took them to an inhabited city.

8   Let them thank Hashem for His lovingkindness and relate His wonders to all of mankind.

9   For He quenched the thirst of the longing soul and filled the hungry soul with good.

10   The ones who are imprisoned in darkness, in the shadow of death, shackled in torment and in iron.

11   For they defied the word of God and scorned the Almighty's counsel.

12   For He humbled their heart with hard labor; they stumbled, with no one to help.

13   Then they screamed to Hashem in agony, and He rescued them from their plight.

14   He took them out from the darkness and the shadow of death and broke their chains of bondage.

15   Let them thank Hashem for His lovingkindness and relate His wonders to all of mankind.

16   For He smashed the prison's brass doors and broke the iron bars open.

17 Fools from following sinful paths were afflicted because of their sins.

18 Their soul abhorred all food, and they reached the verge of death.

19 Then they screamed to Hashem in agony, and He rescued them from their suffering.

20 He sent His word and healed them, saving them from the grave.

21 Let them thank Hashem for His lovingkindness and relate His wonders to all of mankind.

22 And let them slaughter thanksgiving offerings and tell of His deeds in joyful song.

23 The sailors, who travel the sea in ships, who do their work in many waters.

24 They have seen Hashem's deeds and wonders in the depths of the ocean.

25 He commanded and raised a storm wind that lifted the waves up high.

26 The sailors were cast up to the heavens then thrown down to the depths as their souls melted in misery.

PSALM ONE HUNDRED SEVEN

27 They groped and staggered on deck like drunks, and all their nautical skills were of no avail.

28 Then they cried out to Hashem in agony, and He rescued them from their perils.

29 The storm ceased and the ocean became calm, for the waves were stilled.

30 And they rejoiced because the waves became silent, and Hashem led them to their destination.

31 Let them thank Hashem for His lovingkindness and relate His wonders to all of mankind.

32 Let them praise Him amidst a great gathering of people and praise Him in the presence of the elders.

33 He can turn rivers into deserts and water springs into parched land.

34 He turns fertile land into salt flats because of the inhabitants' evil ways.[63]

35 He can turn a desert into a lake and parched land into water springs.

---

63 Refers to destruction of Sodom and Gemorrah, Genesis 19:24

PSALM ONE HUNDRED SEVEN

36   There, He settled the hungry and they built a city to dwell in.

37   And they sowed fields and planted vineyards that yielded plentiful fruit.

38   And He blessed them with many offspring and abundant flocks.

39   But when they sinned, they diminished, subdued in evil and misery.

40   Sometimes Hashem pours contempt on the affluent, making them wander in a wasteland, lost with no apparent way out.

41   But He uplifts the destitute from poverty, enabling them to flourish like flocks of sheep.

42   The righteous see and rejoice while all evil shuts its mouth.

43   Whoever is wise should take note of these things and attentively observe Hashem's loving kindnesses.[64]

---

64   King David's call to take nothing for granted and to avoid being ingrates, preceding Isaiah's subsequent rebuke when the nation failed to do so (see Isaiah 1:3, "My people failed to observe").

PSALM ONE HUNDRED EIGHT

David's thanks to Hashem for overcoming his enemies

1. A song, a psalm by David:

2. My heart is loyal to You, O God; therefore, I will sing and my soul will chant praise.

3. Awake, my soul! Awake, O harp and lyre! I will awaken the dawn.

4. I will thank You among the nations, O Lord; I will sing Your praise among the peoples.

5. For Your compassion is as vast as the heavens, and the truth of Your salvation reaches the uppermost realms.

6. O God, from high in heaven, let Your glory be apparent over all the earth.

7. In order to rescue Your beloved, let Your right hand rescue and answer me.

8. God spoke in His holiness that He would help me and I would rejoice; that I would parcel out Shechem and measure the Valley of Succoth for myself.

9. I will capture the lands of Gilead and Menashe; Efraim will be my stronghold to the north; Judah will be my ministers.

10. Moab will be my wash basin; I'll cast my shoe on Edom; Philistia will be subservient to me.

11. Who will bring me to seize the fortified city? Who will lead me to Edom?

12. Is it not You, O God, who until now has forsaken us, and has not gone forward with our forces?

13. From now on, help us against our adversaries, for human salvation is futile.

14. With God, we will prevail; He will crush our oppressors.

PSALM ONE HUNDRED NINE

A prayer for revenge against enemies

1 For the conductor, a psalm by David: God of my praise, do not be silent.

2 For the evil and the deceitful have opened their mouths; they have spoken the language of falsehood with me.

3 The words of hatred surrounded me, and they fought against me for no reason.

4 In return for my love, they hate me; my only option is to pray to You.

5 They repay me with evil for good and hatred for love.

6 Incite an evil person against him, and may Satan stand at his right side.[65]

7 May he be condemned in judgment and may his prayers be considered a transgression.

---

65 From verses 6-19, David shifts from plural to singular; he is referring to the treacherous Doeg the Edomite, the ringleader of his domestic enemies (see Samuel I, Ch 22).

PSALM ONE HUNDRED NINE

8 May his days be few so that someone else gets his wealth and position.

9 May his children be orphans and his wife be a widow.

10 May his children wander and beg, seeking charity from their hovels.

11 May creditors repossess all that he has; may strangers plunder everything he earns.

12 May no one extend him kindness nor have mercy on his orphans.

13 May his posterity be severed and their names be erased in the next generation.

14 May Hashem be reminded of his fathers' sins and may his mother's guilt not be erased.

15 May they appear to Hashem constantly and may He sever their memory from the earth.

16 For instead of being kind, he pursued a poor and destitute brokenhearted individual on the verge of collapse.

17 Since he loved the curse, it has come to him; since he didn't desire a blessing, it has eluded him.

PSALM ONE HUNDRED NINE

18   He invoked curses upon himself and wore them like a garment; they penetrated his body like water and his bones like oil.

19   Let the curse be like a garment that he wraps around himself and a belt that he always wears.

20   May this be the outcome from Hashem for those who despise me and those who slander me.

21   But You, Hashem, O Lord, act on my behalf for Your Name's sake; rescue me, for Your lovingkindness is good.

22   For I am poor and destitute, and my heart is like a lifeless void within me.

23   I am disappearing like a vanishing shadow; I've been tossed around like a locust.

24   My knees falter from fasting, and my flesh is lean, having lost all its fat.

25   I have become a source of disgrace for them; when they see me, they shake their heads in scorn.

26   Help me, Hashem my God! Save me as befits Your lovingkindness.

27   Let them know that this is Your hand; You, Hashem, have done this.

28 They will curse but You will bless; they rise up but will be humiliated, and Your servant will rejoice.

29 May my adversaries be clothed in guilt and wear their shame like an overcoat.

30 I will exceedingly thank Hashem with my mouth and praise Him amidst the masses.

31 For He stands at the right of the destitute person to save him from those who condemn his soul.

PSALM ONE HUNDRED TEN

Malki Tzedek's song about Abraham, which King David included in his Psalms as an allusion to future wars and the reign of Moshiach

1. A song of praise by David: the word of Hashem to Abraham,[66] my master: "Wait by My right side until I turn your enemies into a footstool at your feet."

2. Hashem will send forth your mighty staff from Zion to rule in the midst of your enemies.

3. Your people will voluntarily join you on the day you go to war, by virtue of your majestic holiness from birth, for your piety from youth is to your credit.

4. Hashem's irrevocable vow is that from you – Abraham – will descend both the priesthood and the monarchy forever, for you have been a righteous king.

5. The Lord is always at your right side; He crushes kings on the day of His anger.

---

66 See Bava Basra 14b and Rashi's commentary there; we respectfully refer to fathers and forefathers as "my master".

6 Hashem will judge the nations as they become a pile of corpses, crushing heads across a vast land.

7 Since he drinks from the river in a certain way, he may proudly lift his head.[67]

---

67 Judges Ch.7 tells of 32,000 men who joined Gideon in his war against Midian. 22,000 were faint-hearted and were sent home. Hashem wanted to show that He wins wars, not the army, and instructed Gideon to go to war with only 300 choice soldiers out of the 10,000 who remained. These were the ones who drank water from the river by cupping their hands and not bending the knee or lying prostrate, indicating that they were holy with no inclination at all toward idolatry.

PSALM ONE HUNDRED ELEVEN

In praise of Hashem

1 Halleluyah! I will thank Hashem with all my heart in the midst of the righteous and among the entire congregation.

2 Hashem's deeds are great, accessible to all who desire them.

3 His works are adorned with glory and majesty, and His righteousness endures forever.

4 He memorialized His wonders; Hashem is gracious and merciful.

5 He provides food for those who revere Him; He remembers His covenant forever.

6 He showed His people the power of His works in giving them the land of nations.

7 Truth and justice are the works of His hands; all His commandments are faithful with no injustice.

8 They are steadfast forever, for posterity, based on truth and fairness.

9   He sent redemption to His people; He commanded His covenant for eternity; His Name is holy and glorious.

10   Reverence of Hashem is the beginning of wisdom; all those who uphold His commandments merit good understanding; His praise endures forever.

PSALM ONE HUNDRED TWELVE

In praise of the pious

1. Halleluyah! Happy is the person who reveres Hashem and deeply desires His commandments.

2. His offspring will be mighty on earth, an upright, blessed generation.

3. Wealth and riches are in his house; his righteousness endures forever.

4. Even in darkness, He shines light on the upright, for He is graceful and merciful and righteous.

5. Good is the person who is gracious and lending, who conducts his affairs justly.

6. For he will never falter; the righteous individual will be remembered forever.

7. He won't fear bad news, for his heart is firm in his trust of Hashem.

8. His heart is steadfast, and he won't be afraid; ultimately, he will see the downfall of those who torment him.

9   He widely distributes charity to the poor; his righteousness endures forever, and his status will be uplifted in honor.

10   The evil person will see this and be angry, gritting his teeth and wasting away in jealousy; the ambition of evil people will perish.

PSALM ONE HUNDRED THIRTEEN

Praise and gratitude to Hashem for His Divine Direction

1. Halleluyah! Servants of Hashem, give praise; praise Hashem's Name.

2. May Hashem's Name be blessed from now on and forever.

3. From sunrise in the east to sunset in the west, Hashem's Name is praised.

4. Hashem towers above the nations; His glory is above the heavens.

5. Who is like Hashem our God, enthroned on high,

6. Who lowers His gaze to oversee heaven and earth?

7. He raises the needy from the dust and uplifts the destitute from the garbage dump,

8. to seat them with noblemen, with the nobles of His people.

9. He transforms the childless wife into a happy mother of children, Halleluyah!

PSALM ONE HUNDRED FOURTEEN

Hashem's revelation at the Red Sea and the Jordan River

1. When Israel left Egypt, the House of Jacob from a people of a foreign tongue.

2. Judah became His sanctuary and Israel His dominion.

3. The sea saw and fled;[68] the Jordan flowed backward.[69]

4. The mountains pranced like rams, the hills like young lambs.

5. What's wrong, O sea; why are you fleeing? O Jordan, why are you going backward?

6. Mountains, why do you prance like lambs? Hills, why like young lambs?

7. Tremble, O earth, in the Lord's Presence, in the Presence of the God of Jacob.

---

68   See Exodus, Ch. 14-15
69   See Joshua, Ch. 3

PSALM ONE HUNDRED FOURTEEN

8 He turns a boulder into a pond of water, a flint rock into a wellspring.[70]

---

70 See Exodus, Ch. 17

PSALM ONE HUNDRED FIFTEEN

Prayer for Hashem to reveal His glory

1. Not for our sake, Hashem; not for our sake, but for the glory of Your Name, reveal Your lovingkindness and truthfulness.

2. Why should the nations scoff, "Where is their God?"

3. But our God is in the heavens and does whatever He desires.

4. Their idols are silver and gold, the product of human hands.

5. They have a mouth, but they don't speak; they have eyes, but they don't see.

6. They have ears, but they don't hear; they have a nose, but they don't smell.

7. They have hands, but no sense of touch; they have legs, but they don't walk; their throats cannot utter a sound.

8. Those who make them will become just like them, and so will anyone who trusts in them.

PSALM ONE HUNDRED FIFTEEN

9   Israel, trust in Hashem! He is their help and protection.

10   House of Aaron, trust in Hashem! He is their help and protection.

11   All of you who revere Hashem, trust in Hashem! He is their help and protection.

12   Hashem, Who always has us in mind, will bless; He will bless the House of Israel; He will bless the House of Aaron.

13   He will bless those who revere Hashem, the young and the old.

14   Hashem will increase blessings upon you; on you, and on your children.

15   You are blessed by Hashem, the Maker of heaven and earth.

16   The heavens are heavens of Hashem, but He has given the earth to mankind.

17   Neither the deceased can praise God nor one who descends to the grave.

18   But we will praise God from now to eternity, Halleluyah!

PSALM ONE HUNDRED SIXTEEN

A prayer for redemption

1. I love that Hashem hears my voice and my prayers.

2. For He turns His ear to me, so I will call Him throughout all my days.

3. When the pains of imminent death encompassed me and the confines of the grave nearly found me, I encountered distress and grief.

4. And I would call Hashem's Name, "Please, Hashem, save my soul."

5. Hashem is forgiving and righteous, and our God is merciful.

6. Hashem protects those who cannot protect themselves; when I was destitute, He saved me.

7. Relax and fear not, my soul, for Hashem bestows goodness on you.

8. For You saved my soul from death, my eyes from tears, and my feet from stumbling.

9. I will walk before Hashem in the land of the living.

PSALM ONE HUNDRED SIXTEEN

10 I held on to my faith, so I spoke to Hashem despite suffering so much.

11 I said in my haste that all mankind is deceitful.

12 How can I repay Hashem for all the goodness He bestows on me?

13 I will raise the cup of salvation and call Hashem's Name.

14 I will pay my vows to Hashem in the presence of all His people.

15 The untimely death of His devoted ones is grievous to Hashem.

16 Please, Hashem, for I am Your servant; I am Your servant, the son of Your maidservant; You have untied the ropes that bound me.

17 I will prepare a thanksgiving offering to You and I will call Your Name.

18 I will pay my vows to Hashem in the presence of all His people,

19 in the courtyards of the House of Hashem in your midst, O Jerusalem, Halleluyah!

PSALM ONE HUNDRED SEVENTEEN

Messianic days

1 Praise Hashem, all you nations; praise Him, all you peoples!

2 For He has overwhelmed us with kindness, and the truth of Hashem is eternal, Halleluyah!

PSALM ONE HUNDRED EIGHTEEN

Thanking Hashem for the future redemption

1. Give thanks to Hashem, for He is good, for His lovingkindness endures forever.

2. Let Israel now declare, "For His lovingkindness endures forever."

3. Let the House of Aaron now declare, "For His lovingkindness endures forever."

4. Let those who revere Hashem say, "For His lovingkindness endures forever."

5. From deep distress, I called out to God; God answered me and brought me relief.

6. Hashem is with me, I will not fear; what can man do to me?

7. With Hashem helping me, I will witness the downfall of my enemies.

8. It is better to take refuge in Hashem than to trust in man.

PSALM ONE HUNDRED EIGHTEEN

9   It is better to take refuge in Hashem than to trust in benefactors.

10 All the nations have surrounded me; in the Name of Hashem, I will obliterate them.

11 They circle around me and surround me; in the Name of Hashem, I will obliterate them.

12 They encircle me like bees, but they'll be extinguished like dry thorns in a fire; in the Name of Hashem, I will obliterate them.

13 My enemies tried to subdue me, but Hashem came to my help.

14 God is my strength and praise, for He has become my salvation.

15 The voice of rejoicing and salvation resounds in the tents of the righteous: "Hashem's right hand is triumphant!"

16 Hashem's right hand is exalted, Hashem's right hand is triumphant.

17 I will not die, for I will live to tell of God's deeds.

18 God has given me extreme tribulations, but He did not let me die.

PSALM ONE HUNDRED EIGHTEEN

19 Open the gates of righteousness for me, so I may enter and give thanks to God.

20 This is the gate to Hashem; the righteous may enter through it.

21 I thank You, for You have answered me and have become my salvation.

22 The stone that the builders rejected has become the main cornerstone.[71]

23 This has emanated from Hashem; to us, it's marvelous.

24 This is the day that Hashem has done; we will rejoice and be happy on it.

25 Please, Hashem, save us now! Please Hashem, bring us success, now!

26 Welcome and be blessed in the Name of Hashem; we bless you from the House of Hashem.

---

71 David's father and brothers rejected him. But, when Samuel the Prophet, came to anoint one of Jesse's sons, no one fathomed that it would be David, who at that time, was out in the field tending the sheep (see Samuel I, 16:4-13). The same imagery applies to Israel, rejected by all the nations, but will become the most honored nation once Moshiach comes.

27 Hashem the Almighty shines His light on us; bind the sacrificial offering with cords to the corners of the altar.

28 You are my God and I will thank You; my God, I will praise You.

29 Give thanks to Hashem, for He is good, for His lovingkindness endures forever.

PSALM ONE HUNDRED NINETEEN

An alphabetical arrangement, eight verses per letter, expressing the desire to serve Hashem wholeheartedly, in every possible way

Aleph

1. Happy are those who walk in the path of innocence and follow Hashem's Torah.

2. Happy are those who observe His commandments and seek Him wholeheartedly.

3. They have done no wrong and follow His ways.

4. You ordered mankind to be meticulous in observing Your commandments.

5. I hope that my ways in life will be conducive to observing Your laws.

6. Then, I won't be ashamed when I look at all Your commandments.

7. I will thank You with a sincere heart as I learn Your righteous statutes.

8. I will observe Your laws, so don't ever abandon me.

Bet

9. How can a young person pursue a path of purity? By observing Your word.

10. I sought You with all my heart; don't let me stray from Your commandments.

11. I guard Your word in my heart so that I will never sin against You.

12. You are blessed, Hashem; teach me Your laws.

13. I have recounted with my lips all the statutes that You declared.

14. I rejoice in the way of Your commandments like a person who obtained uncountable wealth.

15. I will speak of Your commandments and observe Your ways.

16. I will occupy myself with Your laws; I won't forget Your word.

Gimel

17. Be charitable with Your servant; let me live so I can keep Your word.

18. Open my eyes so I can perceive the wonders of Your Torah.

19. I am on this earth for a limited time; don't hide Your commandments from me.

20. My soul is shattered from constant longing for Your statutes.

21. You rebuke the accursed who deliberately stray from Your commandments.

22. Remove disgrace and contempt from me, for I have guarded Your commandments.

23. Even though ministers sat and spoke against me, Your servant is engaged in Torah.

24. Your commandments are both my delight and my trusted guides.

Daleth

25. My soul clings to the dust; revive me in accordance with Your word.

26. I have recounted my ways, and You answered me; teach me Your laws.

27. Let me understand the way of Your precepts so that I can speak about Your wonders.

28. My soul oozes sorrow; sustain me with Your word.

29 Remove the way of falsehood from me and graciously grant me Your Torah.

30 I chose the way of faith; I place Your statutes before my eyes.

31 I cling to Your commandments; Hashem, don't put me to shame.

32 I will run in the path of Your mitzvoth so that You'll give me an understanding heart.

Hey

33 Hashem, teach me the way of Your laws and I will observe them in every possible way.

34 Grant me the understanding to observe Your Torah and I will keep it wholeheartedly.

35 Direct me on the path of Your commandments for that is my desire.

36 Incline my heart to Your commandments and not to the love of money.

37 Divert my eyes from seeing forbidden sights; give me the vigor to follow Your ways.

38 Fulfill Your promise to Your servant that I and my offspring will revere God.

PSALM ONE HUNDRED NINETEEN

39 Remove from me the disgrace of sin that I dreaded, for Your statutes are good and compassionate.

40 See, I yearn for Your commandments; in Your generosity, give me life to fulfill them.

Vav

41 May Your lovingkindness come to me, Hashem; may Your salvation come as You promised me.

42 Then, I can answer those who scorn me, for I trusted in Your word.

43 And do not sever the word of absolute truth from my mouth, for I have longed to truly uphold Your statutes.

44 And I will observe Your Torah always, forever and ever.

45 And I will strive for breadth of understanding, for I sought to grasp Your commandments.

46 And I will speak of Your commandments in the presence of kings, and I won't be ashamed.

47 And I will delight in Your commandments, which I love.

48 And I will uplift my hands to Your commandments, which I love, and I will speak about Your laws.

Zayin

49 Remember Your promise to Your servant, with which You gave me hope.

50 This comforted me in my suffering, for Your promise has kept me alive.

51 Malicious sinners mock me terribly, but I did not deviate from Your Torah.

52 I remembered Your statutes of old, Hashem, and I was comforted.

53 I am horrified because of the wicked who forsake Your Torah.

54 Your laws were like music to me wherever I lived.

55 I remembered Your Name in the time of darkness, Hashem, and I have upheld Your Torah.

56 This, the crown of monarchy[72] has come to me, for I have observed Your commandments.

Het

57 Hashem is my portion; I therefore resolved to uphold His decrees.

---

72 See Tractate Avoda Zara, 44a

58 I have prayed to You with all my heart; be gracious with me as You promised.

59 I evaluated my ways and have directed my feet in the way of Your commandments.

60 I hurried and did not hesitate to keep Your commandments.

61 Gangs of evil people have plundered me, but I have not forgotten Your Torah.

62 I will get up at midnight to thank You for Your just statutes.

63 I am a friend to everyone who reveres You and to those who observe Your commandments.

64 Your lovingkindness fills the earth, Hashem; teach me Your laws.

Tet

65 You have done well with Your servant, Hashem, in accordance with Your promise.

66 Teach me good sense and knowledge, for I believe in Your commandments.

67 Before I agonized myself in Torah, I sinned accidentally; but now, I keep Your word.

68 You are good and do good; teach me Your laws.

69 Evil people spread lies about me, but I observe Your commandments with a whole heart.

70 Their heart became clogged with fat; but for me, Your Torah is my preoccupation.

71 It's good that I suffered hardship, so that I could learn Your laws.

72 The Torah from Your mouth is better for me than thousands of gold and silver ingots.

Yod

73 Your hands made me and prepared me; grant me understanding to learn Your commandments.

74 Those who revere You will see me and rejoice, for I have yearned for Your word.

75 Hashem, I know that Your judgments are just, so rightfully, You made me suffer.

76 May Your lovingkindness console me in accordance with Your promise to Your servant.

77 May Your mercy come to me so I can live, for Your Torah is my delight.

78 May the evil be shamed, for they spread lies about me, but I will speak about Your commandments.

79 May those who revere You and know Your commandments return to me.

80 May I uphold Your laws with a pure heart so that I won't be shamed.

Caph

81 My soul yearns for Your salvation; I hope for the fulfillment of Your promise.

82 My eyes long for Your promise, saying, "When will You comfort me?"

83 Though my skin has become parched from troubles like a waterskin dried in smoke, I haven't forgotten Your laws.

84 How much longer will Your servant live? When will You pass judgment on those who persecute me?

85 The evil dug pits to ensnare me, in violation of Your Torah.

86 All Your commandments are faith; they pursue me with lies; help me!

87 They almost obliterated me from the face of the earth, but I did not forsake Your commandments.

88 In Your lovingkindness, grant me life, so I can uphold Your mouth's decrees.

Lamed

89 Forever Hashem, Your word endures in the heavens.

90 Your faithfulness is from generation to generation; You established the earth and it endures.

91 Heaven and earth stand to this day to do Your bidding, for they all are Your servants.

92 Were it not for my preoccupation with Torah, I would have perished in sorrow.

93 I will never forget Your commandments, for they have kept me alive.

94 I am Yours; save me, for I desire to uphold Your commandments.

95 The wicked hoped to destroy me, but I am engrossed in Your commandments.

96 I have seen an end to every worldly endeavor, but Your commandments are broad beyond limitation.

Mem

97 I love Your Torah so much! It's my discourse all day long.

PSALM ONE HUNDRED NINETEEN

98 Let Your commandments, which I always observe, make me wiser than my enemies.

99 I obtained wisdom from all my teachers, for my discourse is exclusively in Torah.

100 I observe the elders to meticulously fulfill Your commandments.

101 I avoided every evil path to keep Your word.

102 I have not veered from Your statutes, for You have instructed me.

103 Your word is so sweet to my palate, more than honey to my mouth.

104 I ponder Your precepts and therefore despise every false way.

Nun

105 Your word is a candle to my feet and a light unto my path.

106 I have sworn and committed to keep Your righteous statutes.

107 I have been exceedingly afflicted; Hashem, sustain me in accordance with Your word.

108 May the offerings of my mouth be acceptable to You, Hashem; teach me Your statutes.

109 My life is constantly in danger, but I have not forgotten Your Torah.

110 The wicked tried to trap me, but I did not waver from Your commandments.

111 Your commandments are my eternal birthright, for they are the joy of my heart.

112 I have inclined my heart to fulfill Your laws forever, in every way.

Samech

113 I hate those who plot evil, but I love Your Torah.

114 You are my shelter and my shield; I long for the fulfillment of Your promise.

115 Go away from me, you evildoers, and let me guard my God's commandments.

116 Support me in accordance with Your promise and let me live, and don't disappoint my hope in You.

117 Sustain me and I'll be saved, and I will always be engrossed in Your laws.

PSALM ONE HUNDRED NINETEEN

118 You subdue all those who stray from Your laws, for their deceit is a lie.

119 You destroy the wicked of the earth as if they were dross, and therefore, I have loved Your commandments.

120 My flesh shuddered from the dread of You, and I feared Your judgments.

Ayin

121 I practiced justice and righteousness; don't abandon me to those who would wrong me.

122 Be Your servant's guarantor for good, so that malicious people won't wrong me.

123 My eyes look with longing for Your salvation and for the fulfillment of Your promise.

124 Deal with Your servant as befits Your lovingkindness and teach me Your laws.

125 I am Your servant; enable me to understand and know Your Torah and its commandments.

126 It's a time to act for Hashem, for many have abandoned Your Torah.

127 Therefore, I have loved Your commandments more than gold, fine gold.

128 Since all Your commandments are just in my eyes, I've hated every path of falsehood.

Pey

129 The rewards for keeping Your commandments are unfathomable, therefore, I have kept them all.

130 Your opening words illuminate and grant wisdom to the simple.

131 I opened my mouth to swallow the words of Torah because I crave Your commandments.

132 Turn to me and be gracious to me, as is befitting for those who love Your Name.

133 Direct my steps in the path of Your commandments and don't let wickedness dominate me.

134 Save me from human duplicity, and I will observe Your commandments.

135 Shine Your face on Your servant and teach me Your laws.

136 My eyes cry rivers of tears because they did not observe Your Torah.

Tzadi

137 You are righteous, Hashem, and Your judgments are unbiased.

138 You decreed Your commandments in righteousness and in extreme faithfulness.

139 My zealousness and anger consume me, for my oppressors have forgotten Your words.

140 Your word is pure, and Your servant loves it.

141 I am young and disparaged, yet I don't forget Your commandments.

142 Your righteousness is everlasting righteousness, and Your Torah is truth.

143 Trouble and distress have befallen me, but Your commandments are my delight.

144 Your commandments are eternally righteous; give me understanding, and I will live.

Koph

145 I called with all my heart; answer me, Hashem, I will observe Your laws.

146 I called You; save me and I will keep Your commandments.

147 I arose early before dawn and cried out to You; I yearn for the fulfillment of Your promise.

148 I am awake at midnight to converse in Your Torah.

149 Hear my voice as befits Your lovingkindness, Hashem; sustain me in accordance with Your practice.

150 Those who pursue evil schemes are nearing their goals; as such, they have distanced themselves from Your Torah.

151 You are near, Hashem, and all Your commandments are truth.

152 My first knowledge of Your commandments is that You established them forever.

Resh

153 See my affliction and rescue me, for I have not forgotten Your Torah.

154 Fight my fight and redeem me; sustain me so that I can uphold Your Torah.

155 The wicked are far from salvation, for they have not sought Your laws.

156 Hashem, Your mercies are abundant; sustain me in accordance with Your custom.

157 My pursuers and oppressors are numerous, but I did not swerve from Your commandments.

158 I saw traitors and clashed with them because they didn't keep Your word.

159 See how I have loved Your commandments, Hashem; sustain me as befits Your lovingkindness.

160 Your first utterance is truth, and all Your righteous statutes are for posterity.

Shin

161 Noblemen have pursued me for no reason but my heart feared Your word.

162 I rejoice in Your promise like someone who finds an immense treasure.

163 I hated falsehood and loathe it; I have loved Your Torah.

164 I have praised You seven times a day for Your righteous statutes.

165 There is great peace for those who love Your Torah; they encounter no impediments.

166 I hoped for Your salvation, Hashem, and I performed Your commandments.

167 My soul has kept Your commandments, and I love them dearly.

168 I have observed Your commandments and Your precepts, for all my ways are apparent to You.

Tav

169 May my melodious prayer reach You, Hashem; grant me understanding in accordance with Your word.

170 May my prayer come to You; rescue me in accordance with Your word.

171 My lips will speak praise when You teach me Your laws.

172 My tongue will proclaim the words of Your Torah, for all Your commandments are just.

173 My Your hand be ready to help me, for I have chosen Your commandments.

174 I have craved Your salvation, Hashem, and Your Torah is my delight.

175 Let my soul live, and it will praise You, and may Your statutes help me.

176 I strayed like a lost sheep; seek out Your servant, for I have not forgotten Your commandments.

PSALM ONE HUNDRED TWENTY

A prayer for protection against slander and lies

1   A song of ascents;[73] I cried to Hashem in the time of my distress and He answered me.

2   Hashem, save my soul from people who speak the language of lies and the tongue of deceit.

3   What will you gain and what will you benefit, O deceitful tongue?

4   You're like a warrior's sharp arrows; like hot coals from a broom-tree.

5   I grieve for I have been exiled among Edomites, and I have dwelled in the tents of the Ishmaelites.

---

73   In the Holy Temple in Jerusalem, there were fifteen steps that led from the Lower Courtyard to the Upper Courtyard. Psalms 120-134, the fifteen "Songs of Ascents", correspond to these steps. During the daily water procession in Succoth, the Levite singers and musicians would perform each of these songs on the corresponding step as they ascended upwards (Tractate Succah 51b and Rashi).

6 My soul has resided for a long time among those who hate peace.

7 I am for peace, but when I speak, they are for war.

PSALM ONE HUNDRED TWENTY-ONE

A song for strengthening one's trust in Hashem

1. A song of ascents; I cast my eyes to the mountains; from where will my help come?

2. My help comes from Hashem, Maker of heaven and earth.

3. He won't allow your foot to stumble; your Guardian does not slumber.

4. Look, the Guardian of Israel neither sleeps nor slumbers.

5. Hashem is your Guardian; Hashem is your shadow at your right hand.

6. The heat of the sun won't harm you by day, nor the cold of the moon by night.

7. Hashem will protect you from all evil; He will guard your soul.

8. Hashem will guard your departure and your arrival, from now and forever.

PSALM ONE HUNDRED TWENTY-TWO

In praise of Jerusalem

1. A song of ascents, by David: I rejoiced when they said to me, "Let us go to the House of Hashem."

2. Our feet stood within Your gates, O Jerusalem.

3. Once completely built, upper and lower Jerusalem will be a united city.

4. For there, the tribes ascended, the tribes of God, in witness of Israel's purity, to give thanks to the Name of Hashem.

5. For there, sat the thrones of judgment, the Sanhedrin, and the thrones of the House of David.

6. Pray for the peace of Jerusalem and may those who love you[74] live in tranquility.

7. May there be peace within your walls and tranquility within your palaces.

---

74 The second-person pronouns in verses 6-9 refer to Jerusalem.

PSALM ONE HUNDRED TWENTY-TWO

8   For the sake of my brothers and my comrades, I will ask for peace in your midst.

9   For the sake of the House of Hashem, our God, I will pray for your welfare.

PSALM ONE HUNDRED TWENTY-THREE

Yearning for salvation

1. A song of ascents; I cast my eyes to You, Who are enthroned in Heaven.

2. Behold, just as the eyes of the servants look to their master's hand, like the eyes of the maidservant look to her mistress's hand, so do our eyes look to Hashem our God until He graces us with salvation.

3. Be gracious unto us, Hashem, be gracious, for we have suffered so much disgrace.

4. Our souls are replete from the mockery of the complacent and the contempt of the arrogant.

PSALM ONE HUNDRED TWENTY-FOUR

With Hashem's help, we survive

1   A song of ascents, by David: declare now, Israel – were it not for Hashem helping us!

2   Were it not for Hashem being with us when men rose up against us,

3   then they would have swallowed us alive when their wrath burned against us.

4   The floodwaters would have washed us away, and sickness would have plagued our souls.

5   The waters of treachery would have drenched our souls.

6   Blessed is Hashem, Who prevented us from being prey to their teeth.

7   Our soul is like a bird that escaped the hunter's trap; the trap broke and we escaped.

8   Our help is in the Name of Hashem, Maker of heaven and earth.

PSALM ONE HUNDRED TWENTY-FIVE

Hashem's Divine direction during the long and bitter exile

1. A song of ascents; those who trust in Hashem are like Mount Zion, which is immovable and enduring forever.

2. As mountains surround Jerusalem, Hashem surrounds His people, from now and forever.

3. For the rod of evil will not rest on the homeland of the righteous, so that the righteous will not extend their hands to wickedness.

4. Do good, Hashem, to good people and to the righteous of heart.

5. But those who turn to their crooked ways, Hashem will obliterate them with the evildoers; may Israel be in peace.

PSALM ONE HUNDRED TWENTY-SIX

The joy of returning from exile

1. A song of ascents; when Hashem returns the exiles of Zion, we'll be like dreamers.

2. Then, our mouths will be full of laughter and our tongues with songs of joy; then, the nations will say, "Hashem has done great things for them."

3. Hashem has done great things for us; we are overjoyed.

4. Hashem, return our exiles like streams of water in the desert.

5. Those who sow in tears will harvest in joy.

6. Although he walks in the furrow and weeps while planting his seeds, he will surely come in joy when carrying his harvested sheaves.

PSALM ONE HUNDRED TWENTY-SEVEN

A person's success depends on Hashem

1. A song of ascents for Solomon;[75] if Hashem will not build a house, then the construction workers labor in vain; if Hashem doesn't guard a city, then the sentry guards in vain.

2. In vain, do you get up early and toil until late, eating the bread of grief; indeed, He will sustain His beloved who toil in Torah.

3. Take note that children are a gift from Hashem; the fruit of the womb is a reward.

4. Like arrows in the hand of the mighty warrior, so are the children of youth.

5. Fortunate is the man who fills his quiver with them; they won't cower when they encounter their enemies at the gate.

---

75 King David wrote this psalm for his son Solomon, who was destined to succeed him and to build the Holy Temple in Jerusalem.

PSALM ONE HUNDRED TWENTY-EIGHT

Praise of the righteous person

1. A song of ascents; happy is any person who reveres Hashem and walks in His ways.

2. When you eat the fruit of your labor, you are happy and your life is good.

3. Your wife is like a fruitful grapevine within your home and your children are olive saplings around your table.

4. Take note that such is the blessing of a man who reveres Hashem.

5. May Hashem bless you from Zion and may you see the goodness of Jerusalem all the days of your life.

6. And may you see children born to your children, and then peace upon Israel.

PSALM ONE HUNDRED TWENTY-NINE

Condemnation of Israel's oppressors

1. A song of ascents; "Many have oppressed me from my youth," shall Israel say in the time of redemption.

2. Many have oppressed me from my youth, but they could not annihilate me.

3. The plowmen plowed on my back; they made long furrows.

4. Hashem is righteous; He cut the ropes of the wicked.

5. May all those who despise Zion retreat in disgrace.

6. Let them be like the grass on the rooftops that withers even before it's plucked,

7. which the reaper can't even gather a handful or the binder of sheaves an armful;

8. and the passersby will never say, "May the blessing of Hashem be upon you; we bless you in the Name of Hashem."

PSALM ONE HUNDRED THIRTY

A cry for help from the depths of exile

1 A song of ascents; from the depths, I called out to You, Hashem.

2 Lord, hear my voice; may Your ears be attentive to the voice of my pleas.

3 O God, if You take note of my sins and fail to forgive; Lord, who can survive?

4 Yours is the power to forgive so that You'll be revered.

5 I look to Hashem; my soul looks to Him and I yearn for the fulfillment of His promise.

6 My soul awaits the Lord like the guardsmen who await the dawn, those who await the dawn of redemption.

7 Let Israel yearn for Hashem, for Hashem has lovingkindness and the power to redeem.

8 And He will redeem Israel from all its sins.

PSALM ONE HUNDRED THIRTY-ONE

King David's extreme humility

1. A song of ascents by David: Hashem, my heart has not been proud nor my eyes conceited, nor did I pursue anything greater than me and beyond my level.

2. I swear that I have silenced my soul, placing it like a baby in its mother's bosom, so is my soul like a suckling child.

3. Let Israel yearn for Hashem, from now and forever.

PSALM ONE HUNDRED THIRTY-TWO

A psalm about the Davidic Kingdom and building the Holy Temple

1. A song of ascents; Hashem, remember all of David's suffering.

2. How he made an oath to Hashem, a vow to the Mighty One of Jacob.

3. If I enter my royal palace or lie down on the comfortable bed that's prepared for me;[76]

4. if I allow sleep to my eyes or slumber to my eyelids;

5. until I find a place for Hashem, an abode for the Mighty One of Jacob.

6. We heard that it would be in Ephrath, but we found it in the forest fields of Benjamin.

7. We will enter His abode and bow down in the Holy Temple, which is His footstool.

---

76 Verses 3-5 are the content of David's vow in Verse 2, to deny himself the comforts of his own home until he builds the Holy Temple for Hashem.

PSALM ONE HUNDRED THIRTY-TWO

8. Arise, Hashem, to Your resting place, You and the Ark of Your might.

9. Your priests will wear the clothes of righteousness, and Your devoted Levites will sing in joy.

10. For the sake of Your servant David, don't turn away from Your anointed Solomon.

11. Hashem has sworn to David, a truth that He will never go back on, "From your offspring, I will place on your throne."

12. If your sons uphold My covenant and My commandments that I will teach them, then their sons will also sit on your throne till the end of time.

13. For Hashem chose Zion; He desired for it to be His dwelling place.

14. This is My resting place forever; I will dwell here for I have desired it.

15. I will bless her provisions profusely and satiate her needy with bread.

16. I will clothe her priests with salvation and her devoted Levites will always sing in joy.

PSALM ONE HUNDRED THIRTY-TWO

17   There in Zion, will I renew the Davidic dynasty, and I will enable a great light from My anointed Messiah to shine forth.

18   His enemies will be clothed in shame, but upon him, his crown will shine.

PSALM ONE HUNDRED THIRTY-THREE

Brothers living together in Zion

1 A song of ascents by David: how good and pleasant it is when brothers live together in unity.

2 Like the fine oil upon the head dripping down on the beard, the beard of Aaron, that drips down on his garments;

3 just as the dew of Mount Hermon descends on the mountains of Zion, for there, Hashem has commanded the blessing of life forevermore.

PSALM ONE HUNDRED THIRTY-FOUR

Blessing those who rise before dawn to serve Hashem

1. A song of ascents; come bless Hashem, all you servants of Hashem who stand in the House of Hashem during the nights.

2. Lift your hands in holiness and bless Hashem.

3. May Hashem bless you from Zion, Maker of heaven and earth.

PSALM ONE HUNDRED THIRTY-FIVE

The obligation to praise and thank Hashem

1. Halleluyah! Praise the Name of Hashem! Give praise, you servants of Hashem.

2. You who stand in the House of Hashem, in the courtyards of the House of our God.

3. Praise God, for Hashem is good; sing to His Name, for it is pleasant.

4. For God chose Jacob for Himself, Israel as His treasured people.

5. For I know that Hashem is great and that our Lord is above all heavenly powers.

6. For Hashem did whatever He desired in the heavens and on earth, in the seas and in all the depths.

7. He elevates clouds from the end of the earth; He made lightning to bring the rain; He brings the wind from His storehouses.

8. For He smote the firstborn of Egypt, from man to beast.

PSALM ONE HUNDRED THIRTY-FIVE

9   He sent signs and wonders in the midst of Egypt, on Pharaoh and on all of his servants.

10 He smote many nations and slew mighty kings -

11 Sichon, King of the Amorites, and Og, King of Bashan, and all the kingdoms of Canaan;

12 and gave their land as a heritage, a heritage to His people Israel.

13 Hashem, Your Name endures forever; Hashem, Your prominence from generation to generation.

14 For Hashem will judge His people and relent from punishing His servants.

15 The idols of the nations are silver and gold, the handcraft of man.

16 They have a mouth, but they do not speak; they have eyes, but they don't see.

17 They have ears, but they don't hear; they don't even have a breath in their mouths.

18 Those who make them will be just like them, as well as all those who trust in them.

19 O House of Israel, bless Hashem! O House of Aaron, bless Hashem!

20 O House of Levi, bless Hashem; those who revere Hashem, bless Hashem!

21 Blessed is Hashem from Zion, He Who dwells in Jerusalem, Halleluyah!

PSALM ONE HUNDRED THIRTY-SIX

The 26 passages of the psalm correspond to the 26 generations from the creation of the world until receiving the Torah on Mount Sinai, when Hashem sustained the world as a gift, for there was not yet the merit of learning Torah and observing its commandments

1 Give thanks to Hashem, for He is good, for His lovingkindness is everlasting.

2 Give thanks to the God of all the heavenly powers, for His lovingkindness is everlasting.

3 Give thanks to the Lord of the celestial bodies, for His lovingkindness is everlasting.

4 To Him Who alone performs great wonders, for His lovingkindness is everlasting.

5 To Him Who made the heavens with deep insight, for His lovingkindness is everlasting.

6 To Him Who spread the earth upon the waters, for His lovingkindness is everlasting.

7 To Him Who made great lights, for His lovingkindness is everlasting;

8   the sun to dominate the day, for His lovingkindness is everlasting;

9   the moon and stars to dominate the night, for His lovingkindness is everlasting.

10   To Him Who smote the firstborn of the Egyptians, for His lovingkindness is everlasting.

11   And brought out Israel from their midst, for His lovingkindness is everlasting.

12   With a mighty hand and outstretched arm, for His lovingkindness is everlasting.

13   To Him Who split the Red Sea, for His lovingkindness is everlasting;

14   and enabled Israel to pass through it, for His lovingkindness is everlasting;

15   and cast Pharaoh and his army into the Red Sea, for His lovingkindness is everlasting.

16   To Him Who led His people through the desert, for His lovingkindness is everlasting.

17   To Him Who struck down great kings, for His lovingkindness is everlasting.

PSALM ONE HUNDRED THIRTY-SIX

18 And He slew mighty kings, for His lovingkindness is everlasting.

19 Such as Sihon, king of the Amorites, for His lovingkindness is everlasting.

20 And Og, king of Bashan, for His lovingkindness is everlasting.

21 And He gave their land as a heritage, for His lovingkindness is everlasting;

22 a heritage for Israel, His servant, for His lovingkindness is everlasting.

23 When we were downtrodden, He remembered us, for His lovingkindness is everlasting.

24 And He redeemed us from our oppressors, for His lovingkindness is everlasting.

25 He gives food to all flesh, for His lovingkindness is everlasting.

26 Give thanks to the God of the heavens, for His lovingkindness is everlasting.

PSALM ONE HUNDRED THIRTY-SEVEN

A lamenting prophecy about all the exiles; even in exile, one must never forget Jerusalem

1. By the rivers of Babylon, there we sat and also wept when we remembered Jerusalem.[77]

2. On the branches of the willow trees that grew there, we hung the lyres that we played in the Holy Temple.

3. For there, our captors asked us to sing songs, mocking us for their amusement: "Sing us the songs from Zion."

4. How can we sing the song of Hashem on alien soil?

5. If I forget you, O Jerusalem, may my right hand forget its skill.

6. Let my tongue be stuck to my palate if I don't remember you, if I fail to mourn for Jerusalem even at my happiest hour.

---

77 "The Holy One, blessed be He, showed David the destruction both of the first Temple and of the second Temple" (Tractate Gittin 57b). David, in his holy spirit of prophecy, laments the destruction of our Holy Temple even before it was built.

PSALM ONE HUNDRED THIRTY-SEVEN

7   Remember, Hashem, what the offspring of Edom did on the day that Jerusalem was destroyed, when they said, "Burn it, burn it down to the ground!"

8   Daughter of Babylon, you are destined to be plundered; fortunate is the one who repays you in the same way you treated us.

9   Fortunate is the one who smashes your infants against the rock.

PSALM ONE HUNDRED THIRTY-EIGHT

Gratitude for the past and prayer for the future

1. By David: I will thank You with all my heart; I will sing Your praise in the presence of noblemen.

2. I will bow down toward Your Holy Sanctuary and I will give gratitude to Your Name for Your lovingkindness and for Your truth, for You have exalted Your promise even above Your Name.

3. On the day I called You, You answered me; You uplifted me and strengthened my soul.

4. All the kings on earth will acknowledge You, Hashem, for they have heard the words of Your mouth.

5. And they will sing about the ways of Hashem because Hashem's glory is great.

6. For even though Hashem is glorious, He sees the downtrodden; He will humble the haughty from afar.

7. If I walk amidst distress, You revive me, despite my enemies; You send Your hand to destroy them, and Your right hand rescues me.

PSALM ONE HUNDRED THIRTY-EIGHT

8 Hashem, You will grant my wish; Hashem, Your lovingkindness is eternal; don't forsake the works of Your hands.

PSALM ONE HUNDRED THIRTY-NINE

In praise of Hashem's wondrous handiworks

1. For the conductor, by David, a psalm; Hashem, You have scrutinized my heart, and You know that it is pure.

2. You know when I sit and when I stand; you discern my thoughts from far away.

3. You are aware of my walking outside and my reclining at home, and are familiar with all my ways.

4. Before I even uttered a syllable, Hashem, You knew exactly what I wanted to say.

5. You besieged me, front and rear, and You have placed Your hand upon me.

6. Such knowledge defies me; it's beyond my grasp.

7. Where can I hide from Your spirit, and where can I flee from Your Presence?

8. If I ascend to the heavens, You are there; if I descend to the deepest abyss, here You are!

PSALM ONE HUNDRED THIRTY-NINE

9   If I had wings as swift as the light of dawn so that I could dwell on faraway shores;

10   there too, Your hand would guide me, and Your right hand would hold me.

11   If I were to say that I'd hide in the darkness that surrounds me and that the night would conceal me.

12   Not even darkness is dark for You; night and day illuminate identically; darkness and light are the same.

13   You created my mind; You sheltered me in my mother's womb.

14   I thank You for the wondrously glorious way You fashioned me; Your works are marvelous, as my soul knows full well.

15   Even though I was made in concealment, my every bone is apparent to You; I was formed in the lowest parts of the earth.

16   Your eyes saw my unformed limbs, which were all written in Your book; even though they were not yet created, You did not overlook a single one of them.

17   The righteous ones who love You, God, are so precious to me; how prodigious are their deeds!

PSALM ONE HUNDRED THIRTY-NINE

18 If I could count them, they'd outnumber the grains of sand; even in the final generation, I am still with You.

19 O God, if You would only slay the wicked! You bloodthirsty people, get away from me.

20 They invoke Your Name for scheming; Your enemies swear in vain.

21 For indeed, I hate those who hate You, Hashem; I clash with those who rise up against You.

22 I hate them with utmost hatred; they have become my enemies.

23 Scrutinize me, O God, and know my heart; test me and know my thoughts.

24 And see if there's any wrong way in me, and lead me on the way of the everlasting.

PSALM ONE HUNDRED FORTY

A prayer for rescue from informers and slanderous people

1. For the conductor, a psalm by David;[78]

2. Hashem, rescue me from the evil person; protect me from the man of violence;

3. those who devise evil schemes in their hearts and instigate wars every day.

4. They sharpen their tongues like a snake; a spider's venom is forever under their lips.

5. Hashem, guard me from the hands of the evil person and protect me from the man of violence, who conspires to knock me down.

6. The arrogant have set a trap for me with ropes; they spread a net near my footpath and forever place snares along my way.

---

78 This Psalm refers to Doeg the Edomite, who told King Saul that David was plotting with the Cohanim of Nob to revolt (See Samuel I, Ch.22) and the Ziphites, who revealed to King Saul the whereabouts of David in the desert (ibid, Ch. 26).

PSALM ONE HUNDRED FORTY

7   I said to Hashem, "You are my God; Hashem, listen to the voice of my prayers."

8   Lord God, Might of my salvation, You sheltered my head on the day of battle.

9   Hashem, don't grant the desires of the wicked; don't let his plot succeed, or else he'll feel superior forever.

10   Let the head of those who besiege me be buried in the slander of their own lips.

11   Let hot coals of fire descend on them; cast them down to deep pits, never to rise again.

12   Don't let the slanderous individual have a place on earth; may the violent man's own evil hunt him down and subdue him.

13   I know that ultimately, Hashem will champion the cause of the poor, the rights of the destitute.

14   Only the righteous will give thanks to Your Name; the upright will dwell in Your presence.

PSALM ONE HUNDRED FORTY-ONE

A prayer for guarding one's thoughts and tongue

1. A psalm by David: Hashem, I have called out to You; come to me quickly, listen to my voice as I call to You.

2. May my prayer be as acceptable to You as incense and my uplifted hands as an evening sacrificial offering.

3. Hashem, post a sentry on my mouth; guard the door of my lips.

4. Don't let my heart gravitate toward anything evil, to perform evil acts with deceitful sinners and partake of their fancy banquets.

5. May the righteous person chastise me, for his rebuke is lovingkindness; may the oil of anointment never leave my head, for my prayer is that I will never commit the acts of the evil.

6. Their judges have gone astray with hearts of stone; even though they heard my sweet words, they don't repent.

7. Like one who chops wood with chips scattered on the ground, so have our bones been scattered to the mouth of the pit.

PSALM ONE HUNDRED FORTY-ONE

8   My eyes look to You, Lord God, I have sought refuge in You; do not cast my soul away.

9   Protect me from the trap that they laid for me and from the snares of the deceitful sinners.

10   May the evildoers fall into their own traps together until I can pass through safely.

PSALM ONE HUNDRED FORTY-TWO

A plea for help in times of danger

1 A prayer by David, when he was in a cave,[79] retold in contemporary language by a wise orator:

2 I cry out loud to Hashem; I plead to Hashem loudly.

3 I pour out my prayer to Him; I tell Him of my trouble.

4 When my spirit is so tormented, and You know the perils along my path that I walk, they have set a trap for me.

5 Look to the right and see that I have no friend; there is nowhere to escape to and no one cares about me.

6 I cried out to You, Hashem; I said, "You are my shelter; You are all that I have in the land of the living."

7 Listen to my cry in prayer for I have been sorely weakened; save me from those who pursue me, for they are stronger than me.

---

79 For the background on this psalm, see I Samuel, Ch. 24

PSALM ONE HUNDRED FORTY-TWO

8   Free my soul from imprisonment so that I can thank Your Name; in my behalf, the righteous will crown You, because of the kindness You have bestowed on me.

PSALM ONE HUNDRED FORTY-THREE

A continuation of the above plea

1. A psalm by David: Hashem, hear my prayer, listen to my plea; fulfill Your promise to me in Your faithfulness, for You are righteous.

2. Do not judge Your servant according to the letter of the law, for no living being could be exonerated in Your Presence.

3. For the enemy pursued my soul; he crushed my life spirit into the ground; he made me dwell in darkness like those who have been long dead.

4. My spirit is tormented within me; my heart is dumbfounded.

5. I remembered the days of old; I pondered over all Your marvelous actions; I recounted the work of Your hands.

6. I outstretched my hands to You; my soul forever yearns for You like parched land for water.

7. Answer me quickly, Hashem, for my spirit is waning; don't hide Your face from me, otherwise I'll be like those who descend to the grave-pit.

PSALM ONE HUNDRED FORTY-THREE

8 Let me hear Your kindness at the dawn of redemption, for I have trusted in You; show me the path I should take for I cast my soul to You.

9 Hashem, rescue me from my enemies; I have hidden my tribulations from everyone but You.

10 Teach me to do Your will, for You are my God; may Your gracious Divine will lead me along level ground.

11 For Your Name's sake, Hashem, revive me; for the sake of Your righteousness, remove my soul from distress.

12 And in Your lovingkindness, destroy my enemies and demolish all those who oppress my soul, for I am Your servant.

PSALM ONE HUNDRED FORTY-FOUR

Praise and gratitude to Hashem for victories and successes

1. By David: blessed is Hashem, my Rock, Who trains my hands for battle, my fingers for warfare.

2. My Benefactor, my Fortress, my Tower of Strength, my Rescuer; my Shield, in Him I take refuge; He subjugates nations under me.

3. Hashem, what is a man, that You should even pay attention to him, a mortal that You should even think of him?

4. Man is like a breath; his days are like a passing shadow.

5. Hashem, bend Your heavens and descend; touch the kings who are as strong as mountains, and they will erupt in smoke.

6. Flash a lightning bolt and disperse them; shoot Your arrows and vanquish them.

7. Extend Your hands from above; take me out and rescue me from the mighty waters, from the hand of the foreigner;

8. whose mouths speak vanity, and who raise their right hands in false oaths.

9. God, I will sing a new song to You; I will play music for You on a ten-stringed lyre.

10. He Who delivers salvation to the kings, Who rescues His servant David from the evil sword.

11. Take me out and rescue me from the hand of foreigners, whose mouths speak vanity, and who raise their right hands in false oaths.

12. For our sons are like saplings, well-tended in their youth; our daughters are like perfectly-shaped pillars, crafted for a palace.

13. Our storehouses are full, providing from harvest to harvest; our sheep increase by the thousands and ten-thousands, filling our lands.

14. Our cattle are strong; there is no breach, nor transgression, nor shout of anguish in our streets.

15. Happy is the nation who lives like this; happy is the nation that Hashem is their God.

PSALM ONE HUNDRED FORTY-FIVE

Anyone who recites this psalm three times daily is promised a share in the world to come

1. A psalm of praise by David: I will praise You, my God the King, and I will bless Your Name forever and ever.

2. Every day will I bless You and I will praise Your Name forever and ever.

3. Hashem is great and extremely praiseworthy, and His greatness is beyond measure.

4. Generation to generation will praise Your deeds and tell of Your might.

5. I will speak about the majestic glory of Your splendor and Your wondrous acts.

6. People will speak about Your glorious might, and I will tell of Your greatness.

7. They will share recollections of Your great goodness and sing joyfully of Your righteousness.

8. Hashem is forgiving and merciful, patient and tremendously compassionate.

PSALM ONE HUNDRED FORTY-FIVE

9   Hashem is good to all and His mercy is over all His works.

10   All Your works will thank You, Hashem, and Your devout ones will bless You.

11   They will speak about the glory of Your kingdom and talk of Your might,

12   to make His mighty deeds known among people and the glorious splendor of His kingdom.

13   Your monarchy reigns over all the worlds, and Your dominion endures throughout all generations.

14   Hashem supports those who are about to fall and uplifts the downtrodden.

15   All eyes look to You for sustenance, and You give them their food in its proper time.

16   You open Your hand and satiate the desire of every living thing.

17   Hashem is righteous in all His ways and magnanimous in all His deeds.

18   Hashem is close to all who call Him, to all who call Him in earnest.

PSALM ONE HUNDRED FORTY-FIVE

19 He will do the will of those who revere Him; He will also hear their cry and save them.

20 Hashem protects all who love Him, but He will destroy all the wicked.

21 My mouth will speak the praise of Hashem, and may all flesh bless His Holy Name forever and ever.

PSALM ONE HUNDRED FORTY-SIX

The virtue of trusting in Hashem

1. Halleluyah! My soul, praise Hashem!

2. I will praise Hashem as long as I live; I will play music to my God as long as I exist.

3. Don't place your trust in benefactors, in mortals who are powerless on their own.

4. When his spirit departs, he'll return to his plot of earth; on that day, his plans all perish.

5. Fortunate is the individual whom the God of Jacob helps, for he puts his trust in Hashem, his God.

6. For He is the Maker of heaven and earth, the sea and everything in them; He keeps His promise forever.

7. He does justice for the exploited; He gives bread to the hungry; Hashem frees the imprisoned.

8. Hashem gives sight to the blind; Hashem uplifts the downtrodden; Hashem loves the righteous.

PSALM ONE HUNDRED FORTY-SIX

9   Hashem protects the newcomer; He encourages the orphan and the widow but He contorts the way of the wicked.

10   Hashem will reign forever; your God, O Zion, for all generations, Halleluyah!

PSALM ONE HUNDRED FORTY-SEVEN

Wonderful reasons to praise Hashem

1. Halleluyah! For it is good to play music to our God, for it is pleasant and befitting to praise Him.

2. Hashem is the Builder of Jerusalem; He gathers in the exiles of Israel.

3. He heals the brokenhearted and bandages their wounds.

4. He counts the number of stars and gives each one a name.

5. Our Lord is great and extremely powerful; His understanding is immeasurable.

6. Hashem encourages the humble; He lowers the wicked down to the ground.

7. Respond to Hashem with thanksgiving; play music to our God on the lyre.

8. He covers the skies with clouds; He prepares rain for the earth; He makes mountains sprout with fodder.

PSALM ONE HUNDRED FORTY-SEVEN

9   He provides food for the animal, for the young ravens who cry out.

10   He doesn't desire the strength of a horse, nor does He value a man's swift legs.

11   Hashem wants those who revere Him, those who yearn for His lovingkindness.

12   Jerusalem, praise Hashem! Zion, praise your God!

13   For He strengthens the bars on your gates and blesses your children in your midst.

14   He Puts peace on your border; He will satiate you with the cream of wheat.

15   He dispatches His command of rain to earth, which falls quickly to fulfill His word.

16   He gives snow like fleece; He scatters frost like ashes.

17   He throws down His ice like crumbs; who can withstand His cold?

18   He issues His command, and it melts them; His wind blows, and the water flows.

19   He relates His words of Torah to Jacob, His laws and His statutes to Israel.

20 He did not do so for any other nation, for they have not known such statutes. Halleluyah!

PSALM ONE HUNDRED FORTY-EIGHT

A command for all the worlds – upper and lower – to praise Hashem

1. Halleluyah! Praise Hashem from the heavens; praise Him in the heights.

2. Praise Him, all His angels; praise Him, all His legions.

3. Praise Him, sun and moon; praise Him, all the bright stars.

4. Praise Him, the highest of the heavens and the waters that are above the heavens.

5. Let them praise the Name of Hashem, for He commanded, and they were created.

6. He placed them to endure forever, issuing a law of nature that will not change.

7. Praise Hashem from the earth: gigantic sea-creatures and all ocean depths;

8. fire and hail, snow and vapor, storm-wind fulfilling His command;

9. the mountains and all hills, fruit trees and all cedars;

10. wild animals and domesticated animals, insects, and winged birds;

11. kings of the earth and all peoples, ministers and all judges of the earth;

12. young men and also maidens, old men with youths.

13. Let them praise the Name of Hashem, for His Name alone is exalted; His glory permeates earth and heaven.

14. He has exalted the status of His nation, bringing praise for all of His devout ones, for the Children of Israel, the nation that clings to Him. Halleluyah!

PSALM ONE HUNDRED FORTY-NINE

In praise of Hashem Who fights our battles subdues our enemies

1. Halleluyah! Sing a new song to Hashem; His praise is recounted in the congregation of the devout.

2. Let Israel exult in its Maker; the sons of Zion will rejoice in their King.

3. Let them praise His Name with dancing; they will play music to Him on the drum and the lyre.

4. For Hashem desires His nation; He adorns the humble with salvation.

5. Let the pious exult in glory; they will sing in praise on their beds.

6. Lofty praises of God are in their throats and a double-edged sword is in their hand;

7. to take vengeance on the nations, retributions on the peoples;

8. to imprison their monarchs in chains and their noblemen in shackles of iron;

9 to execute the written judgment[80] on them; this is glory for all His faithful, Halleluyah!

---

80 See Ezekiel 25:14

PSALM ONE HUNDRED FIFTY

All of creation should praise Hashem with every breath

1. Halleluyah! Praise God in His Sanctuary; praise Him in the firmament of His power.

2. Praise Him for His mighty acts; praise Him as befits His vast greatness.

3. Praise Him with the blast of the shofar; praise Him with lyre and harp.

4. Praise Him with drum and dancing, with flutes and the oboe.

5. Praise Him with resounding cymbals; praise Him with loud, clashing cymbals.

6. Let every breathing soul praise God, Halleluyah!